Correct Radio Amateur Answers Manual

Table of Contents

Welcome to the N5HZR Correct Radio Amateur Answers Manual (CRAAM). This manual aims to help you pass the 2022 FCC VE Amateur Radio Element 2 Technician test. This is not to be confused with a training guide, an operator's guide, or a how-to document. Once you obtain your Amateur Technician license, you'll need to work hard to learn how YOU want to work with radio.

How to use this document:

One way this process can work is to use the short-term memory we all take for granted. You could plan to take a test some evening and start this process 8 – 10 hours before the test starts. So, let's say the test starts at 6:30 pm. Here is a schedule for the day:

10:00 to 10:45 – Read the **first** segment for 45 minutes.
10:45 to 11:00 – Take a break, hit the restroom, clear your mind.
11:00 to 11:45 – Read the **second** segment for 45 minutes.
11:45 to 12:00 – Take a break, hit the restroom, clear your mind.
12:00 to 12:45 – Read the **third** segment for 45 minutes.
12:45 to 14:00 – Take a break, eat lunch, hit the restroom, clear your mind.
14:00 to 14:45 – Read the **fourth** segment for 45 minutes.
14:45 to 15:00 – Take a break, hit the restroom, clear your mind.
15:00 to 15:45 – Read the **fifth** segment for 45 minutes.
15:45 to 16:00 – Take a break, hit the restroom, clear your mind.
16:00 to 16:45 – Read the **sixth** segment for 45 minutes.
16:45 to 18:30 – Head off to the test site.
18:30 to 19:30 – Relax, take the test.

During each 45-minute reading session, do nothing but read. Turn off all electronic devices. Accept no interruptions. Go somewhere quiet and away from your normal activities.

The CRAAM guide is laid out with each question listed in normal type, and each CORRECT answer listed in **boldface** text. Don't try to guess the answer. Read and remember each question and answer. This is to plant each CORRECT answer in your short-term memory. You are not trying to understand this information; you're trying to remember this information. There's plenty of time to learn how this works AFTER you get up and running. Take your time... You will have almost 8 minutes to read each page.

The NCVEC Question Pool Committee hereby releases into the public domain the 2022-2026 Technician Class, Element 2, Question pool. This pool becomes effective for all Element 2 license examinations administered on July 1, 2022, and is valid until June 30, 2026.

Part 1 – Read this section for 45 minutes…

Which of the following is part of the Basis and Purpose of the Amateur Radio Service?
Advancing skills in the technical and communication phases of the radio art

Which agency regulates and enforces the rules for the Amateur Radio Service in the United States?
The FCC

What do the FCC rules state regarding the use of a phonetic alphabet for station identification in the Amateur Radio Service?
It is encouraged

How many operator/primary station license grants may be held by any one person?
One

What proves that the FCC has issued an operator/primary license grant?
The license appears in the FCC ULS database

What is the FCC Part 97 definition of a beacon?
An amateur station transmitting communications for the purposes of observing propagation or related experimental activities

What is the FCC Part 97 definition of a space station?
An amateur station located more than 50 km above Earth's surface

Which of the following entities recommends transmit/receive channels and other parameters for auxiliary and repeater stations?
Volunteer Frequency Coordinator recognized by local amateurs

Who selects a Frequency Coordinator?
Amateur operators in a local or regional area whose stations are eligible to be repeater or auxiliary stations

What is the Radio Amateur Civil Emergency Service (RACES)?
A radio service using amateur frequencies for emergency management or civil defense communications
A radio service using amateur stations for emergency management or civil defense communications
An emergency service using amateur operators certified by a civil defense organization as being enrolled in that organization
All these choices are correct

When is willful interference to other amateur radio stations permitted?
At no time

Which of the following frequency ranges are available for phone operation by Technician licensees?
28.300 MHz to 28.500 MHz

Which amateurs may contact the International Space Station (ISS) on VHF bands?
Any amateur holding a Technician class or higher license

Which frequency is in the 6 meter amateur band?
52.525 MHz

Which amateur band includes 146.52 MHz?
2 meters

How may amateurs use the 219 to 220 MHz segment of 1.25 meter band?
Fixed digital message forwarding systems only

On which HF bands does a Technician class operator have phone privileges?
10 meter band only

Which of the following VHF/UHF band segments are limited to CW only?
50.0 MHz to 50.1 MHz and 144.0 MHz to 144.1 MHz

How are US amateurs restricted in segments of bands where the Amateur Radio Service is secondary?
U.S. amateurs may find non-amateur stations in those segments, and must avoid interfering with them

Why should you not set your transmit frequency to be exactly at the edge of an amateur band or sub-band?
To allow for calibration error in the transmitter frequency display
So that modulation sidebands do not extend beyond the band edge
To allow for transmitter frequency drift
All these choices are correct

Where may SSB phone be used in amateur bands above 50 MHz?
In at least some segment of all these bands

What is the maximum peak envelope power output for Technician class operators in their HF band segments?
200 watts

Except for some specific restrictions, what is the maximum peak envelope power output for Technician class operators using frequencies above 30 MHz?
1500 watts

For which license classes are new licenses currently available from the FCC?
Technician, General, Amateur Extra

Who may select a desired call sign under the vanity call sign rules?
Any licensed amateur

What types of international communications are an FCC-licensed amateur radio station permitted to make?
Communications incidental to the purposes of the Amateur Radio Service and remarks of a personal character

What may happen if the FCC is unable to reach you by email?
Revocation of the station license or suspension of the operator license

Which of the following is a valid Technician class call sign format?
KF1XXX

From which of the following locations may an FCC-licensed amateur station transmit?
From any vessel or craft located in international waters and documented or registered in the United States

Which of the following can result in revocation of the station license or suspension of the operator license?
Failure to provide and maintain a correct email address with the FCC

What is the normal term for an FCC-issued amateur radio license?
Ten years

What is the grace period for renewal if an amateur license expires?
Two years

How soon after passing the examination for your first amateur radio license may you transmit on the amateur radio bands?
As soon as your operator/station license grant appears in the FCC's license database

If your license has expired and is still within the allowable grace period, may you continue to transmit on the amateur radio bands?
No, you must wait until the license has been renewed

With which countries are FCC-licensed amateur radio stations prohibited from exchanging communications?
Any country whose administration has notified the International Telecommunication Union (ITU) that it objects to such communications

Under which of the following circumstances are one-way transmissions by an amateur station prohibited?
Broadcasting

When is it permissible to transmit messages encoded to obscure their meaning?
Only when transmitting control commands to space stations or radio control craft

Under what conditions is an amateur station authorized to transmit music using a phone emission?
When incidental to an authorized retransmission of manned spacecraft communications

When may amateur radio operators use their stations to notify other amateurs of the availability of equipment for sale or trade?
When selling amateur radio equipment and not on a regular basis

What, if any, are the restrictions concerning transmission of language that may be considered indecent or obscene?
Any such language is prohibited

What types of amateur stations can automatically retransmit the signals of other amateur stations?
Repeater, auxiliary, or space stations

In which of the following circumstances may the control operator of an amateur station receive compensation for operating that station?
When the communication is incidental to classroom instruction at an educational institution

When may amateur stations transmit information in support of broadcasting, program production, or news gathering, assuming no other means is available?
When such communications are directly related to the immediate safety of human life or protection of property

How does the FCC define broadcasting for the Amateur Radio Service?
Transmissions intended for reception by the general public

When may an amateur station transmit without identifying on the air?
When transmitting signals to control model craft

When may an amateur station transmit without a control operator?
Never

Who may be the control operator of a station communicating through an amateur satellite or space station?
Any amateur allowed to transmit on the satellite uplink frequency

Who must designate the station control operator?
The station licensee

What determines the transmitting frequency privileges of an amateur station?
The class of operator license held by the control operator

What is an amateur station's control point?
The location at which the control operator function is performed

When, under normal circumstances, may a Technician class licensee be the control operator of a station operating in an Amateur Extra Class band segment?
At no time

When the control operator is not the station licensee, who is responsible for the proper operation of the station?
The control operator and the station licensee

Which of the following is an example of automatic control?
Repeater operation

Which of the following are required for remote control operation?
The control operator must be at the control point
A control operator is required at all times
The control operator must indirectly manipulate the controls
All these choices are correct

Which of the following is an example of remote control as defined in Part 97?
Operating the station over the internet

Who does the FCC presume to be the control operator of an amateur station, unless documentation to the contrary is in the station records?
The station licensee

When must the station and its records be available for FCC inspection?
At any time upon request by an FCC representative

How often must you identify with your FCC-assigned call sign when using tactical call signs such as "Race Headquarters"?
At the end of each communication and every ten minutes during a communication

When are you required to transmit your assigned call sign?
At least every 10 minutes during and at the end of a communication

What language may you use for identification when operating in a phone sub-band?
English

What method of call sign identification is required for a station transmitting phone signals?
Send the call sign using a CW or phone emission

Which of the following self-assigned indicators are acceptable when using a phone transmission?
KL7CC stroke W3
KL7CC slant W3
KL7CC slash W3
All these choices are correct

Which of the following restrictions apply when a non-licensed person is allowed to speak to a foreign station using a station under the control of a licensed amateur operator?
The foreign station must be in a country with which the U.S. has a third party agreement

What is the definition of third party communications?
A message from a control operator to another amateur station control operator on behalf of another person

What type of amateur station simultaneously retransmits the signal of another amateur station on a different channel or channels?
Repeater station
Who is accountable if a repeater inadvertently retransmits communications that violate the FCC rules?
The control operator of the originating station

Which of the following is a requirement for the issuance of a club station license grant?
The club must have at least four members

Take a 15-minute break!!!!!!!!!!!!!!!!!

Part 2 – Read this section for 45 minutes…

What is a common repeater frequency offset in the 2 meter band?
Plus or minus 600 kHz

What is the national calling frequency for FM simplex operations in the 2 meter band?
146.520 MHz

What is a common repeater frequency offset in the 70 cm band?
Plus or minus 5 MHz

What is an appropriate way to call another station on a repeater if you know the other station's call sign?
Say the station's call sign, then identify with your call sign

How should you respond to a station calling CQ?
Transmit the other station's call sign followed by your call sign

Which of the following is required when making on-the-air test transmissions?
Identify the transmitting station

What is meant by "repeater offset"?
The difference between a repeater's transmit and receive frequencies

What is the meaning of the procedural signal "CQ"?
Calling any station

Which of the following indicates that a station is listening on a repeater and looking for a contact?
The station's call sign followed by the word "monitoring"

What is a band plan, beyond the privileges established by the FCC?
A voluntary guideline for using different modes or activities within an amateur band

What term describes an amateur station that is transmitting and receiving on the same frequency?
Simplex

What should you do before calling CQ?
Listen first to be sure that no one else is using the frequency
Ask if the frequency is in use
Make sure you are authorized to use that frequency
All these choices are correct

How is a VHF/UHF transceiver's "reverse" function used?
To listen on a repeater's input frequency

What term describes the use of a sub-audible tone transmitted along with normal voice audio to open the squelch of a receiver?
CTCSS

Which of the following describes a linked repeater network?
A network of repeaters in which signals received by one repeater are transmitted by all the repeaters in the network

Which of the following could be the reason you are unable to access a repeater whose output you can hear?
Improper transceiver offset
You are using the wrong CTCSS tone
You are using the wrong DCS code
All these choices are correct

What would cause your FM transmission audio to be distorted on voice peaks?
You are talking too loudly

What type of signaling uses pairs of audio tones?
DTMF

How can you join a digital repeater's "talkgroup"?
Program your radio with the group's ID or code

Which of the following applies when two stations transmitting on the same frequency interfere with each other?
The stations should negotiate continued use of the frequency

Why are simplex channels designated in the VHF/UHF band plans?
So stations within range of each other can communicate without tying up a repeater

Which Q signal indicates that you are receiving interference from other stations?
QRM

Which Q signal indicates that you are changing frequency?
QSY

What is the purpose of the color code used on DMR repeater systems?
Establishes groups of users

What is the purpose of a squelch function?
Mute the receiver audio when a signal is not present

When do FCC rules NOT apply to the operation of an amateur station?
FCC rules always apply

Which of the following are typical duties of a Net Control Station?
Call the net to order and direct communications between stations checking in

What technique is used to ensure that voice messages containing unusual words are received correctly?
Spell the words using a standard phonetic alphabet

What is RACES?
An FCC part 97 amateur radio service for civil defense communications during national emergencies

What does the term "traffic" refer to in net operation?
Messages exchanged by net stations

What is the Amateur Radio Emergency Service (ARES)?
A group of licensed amateurs who have voluntarily registered their qualifications and equipment for communications duty in the public service

Which of the following is standard practice when you participate in a net?
Unless you are reporting an emergency, transmit only when directed by the net control station

Which of the following is a characteristic of good traffic handling?
Passing messages exactly as received

Are amateur station control operators ever permitted to operate outside the frequency privileges of their license class?
Yes, but only in situations involving the immediate safety of human life or protection of property

What information is contained in the preamble of a formal traffic message?
Information needed to track the message

What is meant by "check" in a radiogram header?
The number of words or word equivalents in the text portion of the message

Why do VHF signal strengths sometimes vary greatly when the antenna is moved only a few feet?
Multipath propagation cancels or reinforces signals

What is the effect of vegetation on UHF and microwave signals?
Absorption

What antenna polarization is normally used for long-distance CW and SSB contacts on the VHF and UHF bands?
Horizontal

What happens when antennas at opposite ends of a VHF or UHF line of sight radio link are not using the same polarization?
Received signal strength is reduced

When using a directional antenna, how might your station be able to communicate with a distant repeater if buildings or obstructions are blocking the direct line of sight path?
Try to find a path that reflects signals to the repeater

What is the meaning of the term "picket fencing"?
Rapid flutter on mobile signals due to multipath propagation

What weather condition might decrease range at microwave frequencies?
Precipitation

What is a likely cause of irregular fading of signals propagated by the ionosphere?
Random combining of signals arriving via different paths

Which of the following results from the fact that signals propagated by the ionosphere are elliptically polarized?
Either vertically or horizontally polarized antennas may be used for transmission or reception

What effect does multi-path propagation have on data transmissions?
Error rates are likely to increase

Which region of the atmosphere can refract or bend HF and VHF radio waves?
The ionosphere

What is the effect of fog and rain on signals in the 10 meter and 6 meter bands?
There is little effect

What is the relationship between the electric and magnetic fields of an electromagnetic wave?
They are at right angles

What property of a radio wave defines its polarization?
The orientation of the electric field

What are the two components of a radio wave?
Electric and magnetic fields

What is the velocity of a radio wave traveling through free space?
Speed of light

What is the relationship between wavelength and frequency?
Wavelength gets shorter as frequency increases

What is the formula for converting frequency to approximate wavelength in meters?
Wavelength in meters equals 300 divided by frequency in megahertz

In addition to frequency, which of the following is used to identify amateur radio bands?
The approximate wavelength in meters

What frequency range is referred to as VHF?
30 MHz to 300 MHz

What frequency range is referred to as UHF?
300 to 3000 MHz

What frequency range is referred to as HF?
3 to 30 MHz

What is the approximate velocity of a radio wave in free space?
300,000,000 meters per second

Why are simplex UHF signals rarely heard beyond their radio horizon?
UHF signals are usually not propagated by the ionosphere

What is a characteristic of HF communication compared with communications on VHF and higher frequencies?
Long-distance ionospheric propagation is far more common on HF

What is a characteristic of VHF signals received via auroral backscatter?
They are distorted and signal strength varies considerably

Which of the following types of propagation is most commonly associated with occasional strong signals on the 10, 6, and 2 meter bands from beyond the radio horizon?
Sporadic E

Which of the following effects may allow radio signals to travel beyond obstructions between the transmitting and receiving stations?
Knife-edge diffraction

What type of propagation is responsible for allowing over-the-horizon VHF and UHF communications to ranges of approximately 300 miles on a regular basis?
Tropospheric ducting

What band is best suited for communicating via meteor scatter?
6 meters

What causes tropospheric ducting?
Temperature inversions in the atmosphere

What is generally the best time for long-distance 10 meter band propagation via the F region?
From dawn to shortly after sunset during periods of high sunspot activity

Which of the following bands may provide long-distance communications via the ionosphere's F region during the peak of the sunspot cycle?
6 and 10 meters

Why is the radio horizon for VHF and UHF signals more distant than the visual horizon?
The atmosphere refracts radio waves slightly

Which of the following is an appropriate power supply rating for a typical 50 watt output mobile FM transceiver?
13.8 volts at 12 amperes

Which of the following should be considered when selecting an accessory SWR meter?
The frequency and power level at which the measurements will be made

Why are short, heavy-gauge wires used for a transceiver's DC power connection?
To minimize voltage drop when transmitting

Take a 15-minute break!!!!!!!!!!!!!!!!

Part 3 – Read this section for 45 minutes…

How are the transceiver audio input and output connected in a station configured to operate using FT8?
To the audio input and output of a computer running WSJT-X software

Where should an RF power meter be installed?
In the feed line, between the transmitter and antenna

What signals are used in a computer-radio interface for digital mode operation?
Receive audio, transmit audio, and transmitter keying

Which of the following connections is made between a computer and a transceiver to use computer software when operating digital modes?
Computer "line in" to transceiver speaker connector

Which of the following conductors is preferred for bonding at RF?
Flat copper strap

How can you determine the length of time that equipment can be powered from a battery?
Divide the battery ampere-hour rating by the average current draw of the equipment

What function is performed with a transceiver and a digital mode hot spot?
Communication using digital voice or data systems via the internet

Where should the negative power return of a mobile transceiver be connected in a vehicle?
At the 12 volt battery chassis ground

What is an electronic keyer?
A device that assists in manual sending of Morse code

What is the effect of excessive microphone gain on SSB transmissions?
Distorted transmitted audio

Which of the following can be used to enter a transceiver's operating frequency?
The keypad or VFO knob

How is squelch adjusted so that a weak FM signal can be heard?
Set the squelch threshold so that receiver output audio is on all the time

What is a way to enable quick access to a favorite frequency or channel on your transceiver?
Store it in a memory channel

What does the scanning function of an FM transceiver do?
Tunes through a range of frequencies to check for activity

Which of the following controls could be used if the voice pitch of a single-sideband signal returning to your CQ call seems too high or low?
The RIT or Clarifier

What does a DMR "code plug" contain?
Access information for repeaters and talkgroups

What is the advantage of having multiple receive bandwidth choices on a multimode transceiver?
Permits noise or interference reduction by selecting a bandwidth matching the mode

How is a specific group of stations selected on a digital voice transceiver?
By entering the group's identification code

Which of the following receiver filter bandwidths provides the best signal-to-noise ratio for SSB reception?
2400 Hz

Which of the following must be programmed into a D-STAR digital transceiver before transmitting?
Your call sign

What is the result of tuning an FM receiver above or below a signal's frequency?
Distortion of the signal's audio

Electrical current is measured in which of the following units?
Amperes

Electrical power is measured in which of the following units?
Watts

What is the name for the flow of electrons in an electric circuit?
Current

What are the units of electrical resistance?
Ohms

What is the electrical term for the force that causes electron flow?
Voltage

What is the unit of frequency?
Hertz

Why are metals generally good conductors of electricity?
They have many free electrons

Which of the following is a good electrical insulator?
Glass

Which of the following describes alternating current?
Current that alternates between positive and negative directions

Which term describes the rate at which electrical energy is used?
Power

What type of current flow is opposed by resistance?
Direct current
Alternating current
RF current
All these choices are correct

What describes the number of times per second that an alternating current makes a complete cycle?
Frequency

How many milliamperes is 1.5 amperes?
1500 milliamperes

Which is equal to 1,500,000 hertz?
1500 kHz

Which is equal to one kilovolt?
One thousand volts

Which is equal to one microvolt?
One one-millionth of a volt

Which is equal to 500 milliwatts?
0.5 watts

Which is equal to 3000 milliamperes?
3 amperes

Which is equal to 3.525 MHz?
3525 kHz

Which is equal to 1,000,000 picofarads?
1 microfarad

Which decibel value most closely represents a power increase from 5 watts to 10 watts?
3 dB

Which decibel value most closely represents a power decrease from 12 watts to 3 watts?
-6 dB

Which decibel value represents a power increase from 20 watts to 200 watts?
10 dB

Which is equal to 28400 kHz?
28.400 MHz

Which is equal to 2425 MHz?
2.425 GHz

What describes the ability to store energy in an electric field?
Capacitance

What is the unit of capacitance?
The farad

What describes the ability to store energy in a magnetic field?
Inductance

What is the unit of inductance?
The henry

What is the unit of impedance?
The ohm

What does the abbreviation "RF" mean?
Radio frequency signals of all types

What is the abbreviation for megahertz?
MHz

What is the formula used to calculate electrical power (P) in a DC circuit?
P = V x I

How much power is delivered by a voltage of 13.8 volts DC and a current of 10 amperes?
138 watts

How much power is delivered by a voltage of 12 volts DC and a current of 2.5 amperes?
30 watts

How much current is required to deliver 120 watts at a voltage of 12 volts DC?
10 amperes

What is impedance?
The opposition to AC current flow

What is the abbreviation for kilohertz?
kHz

What formula is used to calculate current in a circuit?
I = V / R

What formula is used to calculate voltage in a circuit?
V = I x R

What formula is used to calculate resistance in a circuit?
R = V / I

What is the resistance of a circuit in which a current of 3 amperes flows when connected to 90 volts?
30 ohms

What is the resistance of a circuit for which the applied voltage is 12 volts and the current flow is 1.5 amperes?
8 ohms

What is the resistance of a circuit that draws 4 amperes from a 12-volt source?
3 ohms

What is the current in a circuit with an applied voltage of 120 volts and a resistance of 80 ohms?
1.5 amperes

What is the current through a 100-ohm resistor connected across 200 volts?
2 amperes

What is the current through a 24-ohm resistor connected across 240 volts?
10 amperes

What is the voltage across a 2-ohm resistor if a current of 0.5 amperes flows through it?
1 volt

What is the voltage across a 10-ohm resistor if a current of 1 ampere flows through it?
10 volts

What is the voltage across a 10-ohm resistor if a current of 2 amperes flows through it?
20 volts

In which type of circuit is DC current the same through all components?
Series

In which type of circuit is voltage the same across all components?
Parallel

What electrical component opposes the flow of current in a DC circuit?
Resistor

What type of component is often used as an adjustable volume control?
Potentiometer

What electrical parameter is controlled by a potentiometer?
Resistance

What electrical component stores energy in an electric field?
Capacitor

What type of electrical component consists of conductive surfaces separated by an insulator?
Capacitor

What type of electrical component stores energy in a magnetic field?
Inductor

Take a 15-minute break!!!!!!!!!!!!!!!!

Part 4 – Read this section for 45 minutes…

What electrical component is typically constructed as a coil of wire?
Inductor

What is the function of an SPDT switch?
A single circuit is switched between one of two other circuits

What electrical component is used to protect other circuit components from current overloads?
Fuse

Which of the following battery chemistries is rechargeable?
Nickel-metal hydride
Lithium-ion
Lead-acid
All these choices are correct

Which of the following battery chemistries is not rechargeable?
Carbon-zinc

What type of switch is represented by component 3 in figure T-2?
Single-pole single-throw

Which is true about forward voltage drop in a diode?
It is lower in some diode types than in others

What electronic component allows current to flow in only one direction?
Diode

Which of these components can be used as an electronic switch?
Transistor

Which of the following components can consist of three regions of semiconductor material?
Transistor

What type of transistor has a gate, drain, and source?
Field-effect

How is the cathode lead of a semiconductor diode often marked on the package?
With a stripe

What causes a light-emitting diode (LED) to emit light?
Forward DC current

What does the abbreviation FET stand for?
Field Effect Transistor

What are the names for the electrodes of a diode?
Anode and cathode

Which of the following can provide power gain?
Transistor

What is the term that describes a device's ability to amplify a signal?
Gain

What are the names of the electrodes of a bipolar junction transistor?
Emitter, base, collector

What is the name of an electrical wiring diagram that uses standard component symbols?
Schematic

What is component 1 in figure T-1?
Resistor

What is component 2 in figure T-1?
Transistor

What is component 3 in figure T-1?
Lamp

What is component 4 in figure T-1?
Battery

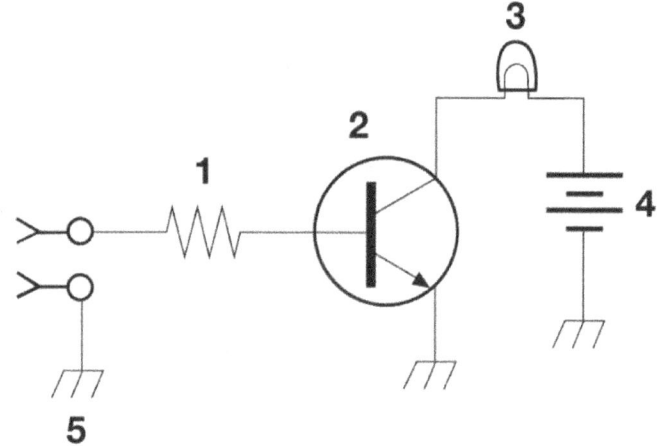

Figure T-1

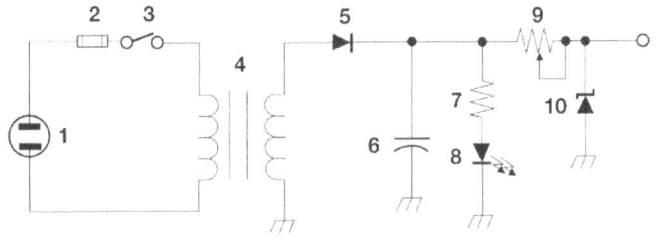

Figure T-2

What is component 6 in figure T-2?
Capacitor

What is component 8 in figure T-2?
Light emitting diode

What is component 9 in figure T-2?
Variable resistor

What is component 4 in figure T-2?
Transformer

What is component 3 in figure T-3?
Variable inductor

What is component 4 in figure T-3?
Antenna

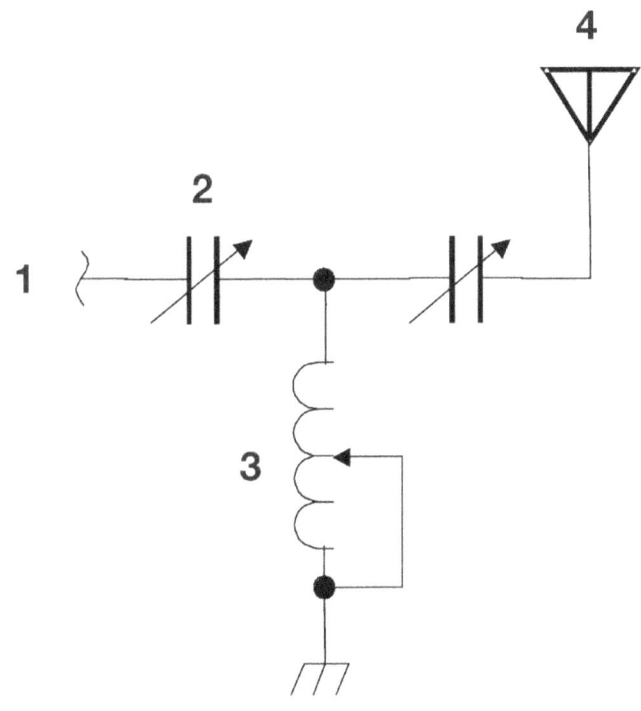

Figure T-3

Which of the following is accurately represented in electrical schematics?
Component connections

Which of the following devices or circuits changes an alternating current into a varying direct current signal?
Rectifier

What is a relay?
An electrically-controlled switch

Which of the following is a reason to use shielded wire?
To prevent coupling of unwanted signals to or from the wire

Which of the following displays an electrical quantity as a numeric value?
Meter

What type of circuit controls the amount of voltage from a power supply?
Regulator

What component changes 120 V AC power to a lower AC voltage for other uses?
Transformer

Which of the following is commonly used as a visual indicator?
LED

Which of the following is combined with an inductor to make a resonant circuit?
Capacitor

What is the name of a device that combines several semiconductors and other components into one package?
Integrated circuit

What is the function of component 2 in figure T-1?
Control the flow of current

Which of the following is a resonant or tuned circuit?
An inductor and a capacitor in series or parallel

Which term describes the ability of a receiver to detect the presence of a signal?
Sensitivity

What is a transceiver?
A device that combines a receiver and transmitter

Which of the following is used to convert a signal from one frequency to another?
Mixer

Which term describes the ability of a receiver to discriminate between multiple signals?
Selectivity

What is the name of a circuit that generates a signal at a specific frequency?
Oscillator

What device converts the RF input and output of a transceiver to another band?
Transverter

What is the function of a transceiver's PTT input?
Switches transceiver from receive to transmit when grounded

Which of the following describes combining speech with an RF carrier signal?
Modulation

What is the function of the SSB/CW-FM switch on a VHF power amplifier?
Set the amplifier for proper operation in the selected mode

What device increases the transmitted output power from a transceiver?
An RF power amplifier

Where is an RF preamplifier installed?
Between the antenna and receiver

What can you do if you are told your FM handheld or mobile transceiver is over-deviating?
Talk farther away from the microphone

What would cause a broadcast AM or FM radio to receive an amateur radio transmission unintentionally?
The receiver is unable to reject strong signals outside the AM or FM band

Which of the following can cause radio frequency interference?
Fundamental overload
Harmonics
Spurious emissions
All these choices are correct

Which of the following could you use to cure distorted audio caused by RF current on the shield of a microphone cable?
Ferrite choke

How can fundamental overload of a non-amateur radio or TV receiver by an amateur signal be reduced or eliminated?
Block the amateur signal with a filter at the antenna input of the affected receiver

Which of the following actions should you take if a neighbor tells you that your station's transmissions are interfering with their radio or TV reception?
Make sure that your station is functioning properly and that it does not cause interference to your own radio or television when it is tuned to the same channel

Which of the following can reduce overload of a VHF transceiver by a nearby commercial FM station?
Installing a band-reject filter

What should you do if something in a neighbor's home is causing harmful interference to your amateur station?
Work with your neighbor to identify the offending device
Politely inform your neighbor that FCC rules prohibit the use of devices that cause interference
Make sure your station meets the standards of good amateur practice
All these choices are correct

What should be the first step to resolve non-fiber optic cable TV interference caused by your amateur radio transmission?
Be sure all TV feed line coaxial connectors are installed properly

What might be a problem if you receive a report that your audio signal through an FM repeater is distorted or unintelligible?
Your transmitter is slightly off frequency
Your batteries are running low
You are in a bad location
All these choices are correct

What is a symptom of RF feedback in a transmitter or transceiver?
Reports of garbled, distorted, or unintelligible voice transmissions

What is the primary purpose of a dummy load?
To prevent transmitting signals over the air when making tests

Which of the following is used to determine if an antenna is resonant at the desired operating frequency?
An antenna analyzer

What does a dummy load consist of?
A non-inductive resistor mounted on a heat sink

Take a 15-minute break!!!!!!!!!!!!!!!!

Part 5 – Read this section for 45 minutes…

What reading on an SWR meter indicates a perfect impedance match between the antenna and the feed line?
1:1

Why do most solid-state transmitters reduce output power as SWR increases beyond a certain level?
To protect the output amplifier transistors

What does an SWR reading of 4:1 indicate?
Impedance mismatch

What happens to power lost in a feed line?
It is converted into heat

Which instrument can be used to determine SWR?
Directional wattmeter

Which of the following causes failure of coaxial cables?
Moisture contamination

Why should the outer jacket of coaxial cable be resistant to ultraviolet light?
Ultraviolet light can damage the jacket and allow water to enter the cable

What is a disadvantage of air core coaxial cable when compared to foam or solid dielectric types?
It requires special techniques to prevent moisture in the cable

Which instrument would you use to measure electric potential?
A voltmeter

How is a voltmeter connected to a component to measure applied voltage?
In parallel

When configured to measure current, how is a multimeter connected to a component?
In series

Which instrument is used to measure electric current?
An ammeter

Which of the following can damage a multimeter?
Attempting to measure voltage when using the resistance setting

Which of the following measurements are made using a multimeter?
Voltage and resistance

Which of the following types of solder should not be used for radio and electronic applications?
Acid-core solder

What is the characteristic appearance of a cold tin-lead solder joint?
A rough or lumpy surface

What reading indicates that an ohmmeter is connected across a large, discharged capacitor?
Increasing resistance with time

Which of the following precautions should be taken when measuring in-circuit resistance with an ohmmeter?
Ensure that the circuit is not powered

Which of the following is a form of amplitude modulation?
Single sideband

What type of modulation is commonly used for VHF packet radio transmissions?
FM or PM

Which type of voice mode is often used for long-distance (weak signal) contacts on the VHF and UHF bands?
SSB

Which type of modulation is commonly used for VHF and UHF voice repeaters?
FM or PM

Which of the following types of signal has the narrowest bandwidth?
CW

Which sideband is normally used for 10 meter HF, VHF, and UHF single-sideband communications?
Upper sideband

What is a characteristic of single sideband (SSB) compared to FM?
SSB signals have narrower bandwidth

What is the approximate bandwidth of a typical single sideband (SSB) voice signal?
3 kHz

What is the approximate bandwidth of a VHF repeater FM voice signal?
Between 10 and 15 kHz

What is the approximate bandwidth of AM fast-scan TV transmissions?
About 6 MHz

What is the approximate bandwidth required to transmit a CW signal?
150 Hz

Which of the following is a disadvantage of FM compared with single sideband?
Only one signal can be received at a time

What telemetry information is typically transmitted by satellite beacons?
Health and status of the satellite

What is the impact of using excessive effective radiated power on a satellite uplink?
Blocking access by other users

Which of the following are provided by satellite tracking programs?
Maps showing the real-time position of the satellite track over Earth
The time, azimuth, and elevation of the start, maximum altitude, and end of a pass
The apparent frequency of the satellite transmission, including effects of Doppler shift
All these choices are correct

What mode of transmission is commonly used by amateur radio satellites?
SSB
FM
CW/data
All these choices are correct

What is a satellite beacon?
A transmission from a satellite that contains status information

Which of the following are inputs to a satellite tracking program?
The Keplerian elements

What is Doppler shift in reference to satellite communications?
An observed change in signal frequency caused by relative motion between the satellite and Earth station

What is meant by the statement that a satellite is operating in U/V mode?
The satellite uplink is in the 70 centimeter band and the downlink is in the 2 meter band

What causes spin fading of satellite signals?
Rotation of the satellite and its antennas

What is a LEO satellite?
A satellite in low earth orbit

Who may receive telemetry from a space station?
Anyone

Which of the following is a way to determine whether your satellite uplink power is neither too low nor too high?
Your signal strength on the downlink should be about the same as the beacon

Which of the following methods is used to locate sources of noise interference or jamming?
Radio direction finding

Which of these items would be useful for a hidden transmitter hunt?
A directional antenna

What operating activity involves contacting as many stations as possible during a specified period?
Contesting

Which of the following is good procedure when contacting another station in a contest?
Send only the minimum information needed for proper identification and the contest exchange

What is a grid locator?
A letter-number designator assigned to a geographic location

How is over the air access to IRLP nodes accomplished?
By using DTMF signals

What is Voice Over Internet Protocol (VoIP)?
A method of delivering voice communications over the internet using digital techniques

What is the Internet Radio Linking Project (IRLP)?
A technique to connect amateur radio systems, such as repeaters, via the internet using Voice Over Internet Protocol (VoIP)

Which of the following protocols enables an amateur station to transmit through a repeater without using a radio to initiate the transmission?
EchoLink

What is required before using the EchoLink system?
Register your call sign and provide proof of license

What is an amateur radio station that connects other amateur stations to the internet?
A gateway

Which of the following is a digital communications mode?
Packet radio
IEEE 802.11
FT8
All these choices are correct

What is a "talkgroup" on a digital repeater?
A way for groups of users to share a channel at different times without hearing other users on the channel

What kind of data can be transmitted by APRS?
GPS position data
Text messages
Weather data
All these choices are correct

What type of transmission is indicated by the term "NTSC?"
An analog fast-scan color TV signal

Which of the following is an application of APRS?
Providing real-time tactical digital communications in conjunction with a map showing the locations of stations

What does the abbreviation "PSK" mean?
Phase Shift Keying

Which of the following describes DMR?
A technique for time-multiplexing two digital voice signals on a single 12.5 kHz repeater channel

Which of the following is included in packet radio transmissions?
A check sum that permits error detection
A header that contains the call sign of the station to which the information is being sent
Automatic repeat request in case of error
All these choices are correct

What is CW?
Another name for a Morse code transmission

Which of the following operating activities is supported by digital mode software in the WSJT-X software suite?
Earth-Moon-Earth
Weak signal propagation beacons
Meteor scatter
All these choices are correct

What is an ARQ transmission system?
An error correction method in which the receiving station detects errors and sends a request for retransmission

Which of the following best describes an amateur radio mesh network?
An amateur-radio based data network using commercial Wi-Fi equipment with modified firmware

What is FT8?
A digital mode capable of low signal-to-noise operation

What is a beam antenna?
An antenna that concentrates signals in one direction

Which of the following describes a type of antenna loading?
Electrically lengthening by inserting inductors in radiating elements

Which of the following describes a simple dipole oriented parallel to Earth's surface?
A horizontally polarized antenna

What is a disadvantage of the short, flexible antenna supplied with most handheld radio transceivers, compared to a full-sized quarter-wave antenna?
It has low efficiency

Take a 15-minute break!!!!!!!!!!!!!!!

Part 6 – Read this section for 45 minutes…

Which of the following increases the resonant frequency of a dipole antenna?
Shortening it

Which of the following types of antenna offers the greatest gain?
Yagi

What is a disadvantage of using a handheld VHF transceiver with a flexible antenna inside a vehicle?
Signal strength is reduced due to the shielding effect of the vehicle

What is the approximate length, in inches, of a quarter-wavelength vertical antenna for 146 MHz?
19

What is the approximate length, in inches, of a half-wavelength 6 meter dipole antenna?
112

In which direction does a half-wave dipole antenna radiate the strongest signal?
In the direction of the feed line

What is antenna gain?
The increase in signal strength in a specified direction compared to a reference antenna

What is an advantage of a 5/8 wavelength whip antenna for VHF or UHF mobile service?
It has more gain than a 1/4-wavelength antenna

What is a benefit of low SWR?
Reduced signal loss

What is the most common impedance of coaxial cables used in amateur radio?
50 ohms

Why is coaxial cable the most common feed line for amateur radio antenna systems?
It is easy to use and requires few special installation considerations

What is the major function of an antenna tuner (antenna coupler)?
It matches the antenna system impedance to the transceiver's output impedance

What happens as the frequency of a signal in coaxial cable is increased?
The loss increases

Which of the following RF connector types is most suitable for frequencies above 400 MHz?
Type N

Which of the following is true of PL-259 type coax connectors?
They are commonly used at HF and VHF frequencies

Which of the following is a source of loss in coaxial feed line?
Water intrusion into coaxial connectors
High SWR
Multiple connectors in the line
All these choices are correct

What can cause erratic changes in SWR?
Loose connection in the antenna or feed line

What is the electrical difference between RG-58 and RG-213 coaxial cable?
RG-213 cable has less loss at a given frequency

Which of the following types of feed line has the lowest loss at VHF and UHF?
Air-insulated hardline

What is standing wave ratio (SWR)?
A measure of how well a load is matched to a transmission line

Which of the following is a safety hazard of a 12-volt storage battery?
Shorting the terminals can cause burns, fire, or an explosion

What health hazard is presented by electrical current flowing through the body?
It may cause injury by heating tissue
It may disrupt the electrical functions of cells
It may cause involuntary muscle contractions
All these choices are correct

In the United States, what circuit does black wire insulation indicate in a three-wire 120 V cable?
Hot

What is the purpose of a fuse in an electrical circuit?
To remove power in case of overload

Why should a 5-ampere fuse never be replaced with a 20-ampere fuse?
Excessive current could cause a fire

What is a good way to guard against electrical shock at your station?
Use three-wire cords and plugs for all AC powered equipment
Connect all AC powered station equipment to a common safety ground
Install mechanical interlocks in high-voltage circuits
All these choices are correct

Where should a lightning arrester be installed in a coaxial feed line?
On a grounded panel near where feed lines enter the building

Where should a fuse or circuit breaker be installed in a 120V AC power circuit?
In series with the hot conductor only

What should be done to all external ground rods or earth connections?
Bond them together with heavy wire or conductive strap

What hazard is caused by charging or discharging a battery too quickly?
Overheating or out-gassing

What hazard exists in a power supply immediately after turning it off?
Charge stored in filter capacitors

Which of the following precautions should be taken when measuring high voltages with a voltmeter?
Ensure that the voltmeter and leads are rated for use at the voltages to be measured

Which of the following is good practice when installing ground wires on a tower for lightning protection?
Ensure that connections are short and direct

What is required when climbing an antenna tower?
Have sufficient training on safe tower climbing techniques
Use appropriate tie-off to the tower at all times
Always wear an approved climbing harness
All these choices are correct

Under what circumstances is it safe to climb a tower without a helper or observer?
Never

Which of the following is an important safety precaution to observe when putting up an antenna tower?
Look for and stay clear of any overhead electrical wires

What is the purpose of a safety wire through a turnbuckle used to tension guy lines?
Prevent loosening of the turnbuckle from vibration

What is the minimum safe distance from a power line to allow when installing an antenna?
Enough so that if the antenna falls, no part of it can come closer than 10 feet to the power wires

Which of the following is an important safety rule to remember when using a crank-up tower?
This type of tower must not be climbed unless it is retracted, or mechanical safety locking devices have been installed

Which is a proper grounding method for a tower?
Separate eight-foot ground rods for each tower leg, bonded to the tower and each other

Why should you avoid attaching an antenna to a utility pole?
The antenna could contact high-voltage power lines

Which of the following is true when installing grounding conductors used for lightning protection?
Sharp bends must be avoided

Which of the following establishes grounding requirements for an amateur radio tower or antenna?
Local electrical codes

What type of radiation are radio signals?
Non-ionizing radiation

At which of the following frequencies does maximum permissible exposure have the lowest value?
50 MHz

How does the allowable power density for RF safety change if duty cycle changes from 100 percent to 50 percent?
It increases by a factor of 2

What factors affect the RF exposure of people near an amateur station antenna?
Frequency and power level of the RF field
Distance from the antenna to a person
Radiation pattern of the antenna
All these choices are correct

Why do exposure limits vary with frequency?
The human body absorbs more RF energy at some frequencies than at others

Which of the following is an acceptable method to determine whether your station complies with FCC RF exposure regulations?
By calculation based on FCC OET Bulletin 65
By calculation based on computer modeling
By measurement of field strength using calibrated equipment
All these choices are correct

What hazard is created by touching an antenna during a transmission?
RF burn to skin

Which of the following actions can reduce exposure to RF radiation?
Relocate antennas

How can you make sure your station stays in compliance with RF safety regulations?
By re-evaluating the station whenever an item in the transmitter or antenna system is changed

Why is duty cycle one of the factors used to determine safe RF radiation exposure levels?
It affects the average exposure to radiation

What is the definition of duty cycle during the averaging time for RF exposure?
The percentage of time that a transmitter is transmitting

How does RF radiation differ from ionizing radiation (radioactivity)?
RF radiation does not have sufficient energy to cause chemical changes in cells and damage DNA

Who is responsible for ensuring that no person is exposed to RF energy above the FCC exposure limits?
The station licensee

Ready for Test!!!!!!!!!!!!!!!!

Welcome to the N5HZR Correct Radio Amateur Answers Manual (CRAAM). The goal of this manual is to help you pass the 2023 FCC VE Amateur Radio Element 3, General test. This is not to be confused with a training guide, an operator's guide, or a how-to document. Once you obtain your Amateur General license, you'll need to work hard to learn how YOU want to work with radio.

How to use this document:

One way this process can work is to use the short-term memory we all take for granted. You could plan to take a test some evening and start this process 8 – 10 hours before the test starts. So, let's say the test starts at 6:30 pm. Here is a schedule for the day:

10:00 to 10:45 – Read the **first** segment for 45 minutes.
10:45 to 11:00 – Take a break, hit the restroom, clear your mind.
11:00 to 11:45 – Read the **second** segment for 45 minutes.
11:45 to 12:00 – Take a break, hit the restroom, clear your mind.
12:00 to 12:45 – Read the **third** segment for 45 minutes.
12:45 to 14:00 – Take a break, eat lunch, hit the restroom, clear your mind.
14:00 to 14:45 – Read the **fourth** segment for 45 minutes.
14:45 to 15:00 – Take a break, hit the restroom, clear your mind.
15:00 to 15:45 – Read the **fifth** segment for 45 minutes.
15:45 to 16:00 – Take a break, hit the restroom, clear your mind.
16:00 to 16:45 – Read the **sixth** segment for 45 minutes.
16:45 to 18:30 – Head off to the test site.
18:30 to 19:30 – Relax, take the test.

During each 45-minute reading session, do nothing but rea Turn off all electronic devices. Accept no interruptions. Go somewhere quiet, and away from your normal activities.

The CRAAM guide is laid out with each question listed in normal type, and each CORRECT answer listed in **boldface** text. Don't try to guess the answer. Read and remember each question and answer. This is to plant each CORRECT answer in your short-term memory. You are not trying to understand this information; you're trying to remember it. There's plenty of time to learn how this works AFTER you get up and running. Take your time... You will have almost 6.5 minutes to read each page.

This pool becomes effective for all Element 3 examinations to be administered on July 1, 2023, and remains valid until June 30, 2027.

Part 1 – Read this section for 45 minutes...

On which HF and/or MF amateur bands are there portions where General class licensees cannot transmit?
80 meters, 40 meters, 20 meters, and 15 meters

On which of the following bands is phone operation prohibited?
30 meters

On which of the following bands is image transmission prohibited?
30 meters

Which of the following amateur bands is restricted to communication only on specific channels, rather than frequency ranges?
60 meters

On which of the following frequencies are General class licensees prohibited from operating as control operator?
7.125 MHz to 7.175 MHz

Which of the following applies when the FCC rules designate the amateur service as a secondary user on a band?
Amateur stations must not cause harmful interference to primary users and must accept interference from primary users

On which amateur frequencies in the 10-meter band may stations with a General class control operator transmit CW emissions?
The entire band

Which HF bands have segments exclusively allocated to Amateur Extra licensees?
80 meters, 40 meters, 20 meters, and 15 meters

Which of the following frequencies is within the General class portion of the 15-meter band?
21300 kHz

What portion of the 10-meter band is available for repeater use?
The portion above 29.5 MHz

When General class licensees are not permitted to use the entire voice portion of a band, which portion of the voice segment is available to them?
The upper frequency portion

What is the maximum height above ground for an antenna structure near a public use airport without requiring notification to the FAA and registration with the FCC?
200 feet

With which of the following conditions must beacon stations comply?
No more than one beacon station may transmit in the same band from the same station location

Which of the following is a purpose of a beacon station as identified in the FCC rules?
Observation of propagation and reception

Which of the following transmissions is permitted for all amateur stations?
Occasional retransmission of weather and propagation forecast information from US government stations

Which of the following one-way transmissions are permitted?
Transmissions to assist with learning the International Morse code

Under what conditions are state and local governments permitted to regulate amateur radio antenna structures?
Amateur Service communications must be reasonably accommodated, and regulations must constitute the minimum practical to accommodate a legitimate purpose of the state or local entity

What are the restrictions on the use of abbreviations or procedural signals in the amateur service?
They may be used if they do not obscure the meaning of a message

When is it permissible to communicate with amateur stations in countries outside the areas administered by the Federal Communications Commission?
When the contact is with amateurs in any country except those whose administrations have notified the ITU that they object to such communications

On what HF frequencies are automatically controlled beacons permitted?
28.20 MHz to 28.30 MHz

What is the power limit for beacon stations?
100 watts PEP output

Who or what determines "good engineering and good amateur practice," as applied to the operation of an amateur station in all respects not covered by the Part 97 rules?
The FCC

What is the maximum transmitting power an amateur station may use on 10.140 MHz?
200 watts PEP output

What is the maximum transmitting power an amateur station may use on the 12-meter band?
1500 watts PEP output

What is the maximum bandwidth permitted by FCC rules for amateur radio stations transmitting on USB frequencies in the 60-meter band?
2.8 kHz

Which of the following is required by the FCC rules when operating in the 60-meter band?
If you are using an antenna other than a dipole, you must keep a record of the gain of your antenna

What is the limit for transmitter power on the 28 MHz band for a General Class control operator?
1500 watts PEP output

What is the limit for transmitter power on the 1.8 MHz band?
1500 watts PEP output

What must be done before using a new digital protocol on the air?
Publicly document the technical characteristics of the protocol

What is the maximum power limit on the 60-meter band?
ERP of 100 watts PEP with respect to a dipole

What measurement is specified by FCC rules that regulate maximum power?
PEP output from the transmitter

Who may receive partial credit for the elements represented by an expired amateur radio license?
Any person who can demonstrate that they once held an FCC-issued General, Advanced, or Amateur Extra class license that was not revoked by the FCC

What license examinations may you administer as an accredited Volunteer Examiner holding a General class operator license?
Technician only

On which of the following band segments may you operate if you are a Technician class operator and have an unexpired Certificate of Successful Completion of Examination (CSCE) for General class privileges?
On any General or Technician class band segment

Who must observe the administration of a Technician class license examination?
At least three Volunteer Examiners of General class or higher

When operating a US station by remote control from outside the country, what license is required of the control operator?
A US operator/primary station license

Until an upgrade to General class is shown in the FCC database, when must a Technician licensee identify with "AG" after their call sign?
Whenever they operate using General class frequency privileges

Volunteer Examiners are accredited by what organization?
A Volunteer Examiner Coordinator

Which of the following criteria must be met for a non-US citizen to be an accredited Volunteer Examiner?
The person must hold an FCC granted amateur radio license of General class or above

How long is a Certificate of Successful Completion of Examination (CSCE) valid for exam element credit?
365 days

What is the minimum age that one must be to qualify as an accredited Volunteer Examiner?
18 years

What action is required to obtain a new General class license after a previously held license has expired and the two-year grace period has passed?
The applicant must show proof of the appropriate expired license grant and pass the current Element 2 exam

When operating a station in South America by remote control over the internet from the US, what regulations apply?
Only those of the remote station's country

Which of the following would disqualify a third party from participating in sending a message via an amateur station?
The third party's amateur license has been revoked and not reinstated

When may a 10-meter repeater retransmit the 2-meter signal from a station that has a Technician class control operator?
Only if the 10-meter repeater control operator holds at least a General class license

What is required to conduct communications with a digital station operating under automatic control outside the automatic control band segments?
The station initiating the contact must be under local or remote control

Which of the following conditions require a licensed amateur radio operator to take specific steps to avoid harmful interference to other users or facilities?
When operating within one mile of an FCC Monitoring Station
When using a band where the Amateur Service is secondary
When a station is transmitting spread spectrum emissions
All these choices are correct

What are the restrictions on messages sent to a third party in a country with which there is a Third-Party Agreement?
They must relate to amateur radio, or remarks of a personal character, or messages relating to emergencies or disaster relief

The frequency allocations of which ITU region apply to radio amateurs operating in North and South America?
Region 2

In what part of the 2.4 GHz band may an amateur station communicate with non-licensed Wi-Fi stations?
No part

What is the maximum PEP output allowed for spread spectrum transmissions?
10 watts

Under what circumstances are messages that are sent via digital modes exempt from Part 97 third-party rules that apply to other modes of communication?
Under no circumstances

Why should an amateur operator normally avoid transmitting on 14.100, 18.110, 21.150, 24. 930 and 28.200 MHz?
A system of propagation beacon stations operates on those frequencies

On what bands may automatically controlled stations transmitting RTTY or data emissions communicate with other automatically controlled digital stations?
Anywhere in the 6-meter or shorter wavelength bands, and in limited segments of some of the HF bands

When may third-party messages be transmitted via remote control?
Under any circumstances in which third party messages are permitted by FCC rules

Which mode is most commonly used for voice communications on frequencies of 14 MHz or higher?
Upper sideband

Which mode is most commonly used for voice communications on the 160-, 75-, and 40-meter bands?
Lower sideband

Which mode is most commonly used for SSB voice communications in the VHF and UHF bands?
Upper sideband

Which mode is most commonly used for voice communications on the 17- and 12-meter bands?
Upper sideband

Which mode of voice communication is most commonly used on the HF amateur bands?
Single sideband

Which of the following is an advantage of using single sideband, as compared to other analog voice modes on the HF amateur bands?
Less bandwidth used and greater power efficiency

Which of the following statements is true of single sideband (SSB)?
Only one sideband is transmitted; the other sideband and carrier are suppressed

What is the recommended way to break into a phone contact?
Say your call sign once

Why do most amateur stations use lower sideband on the 160-, 75-, and 40-meter bands?
It is commonly accepted amateur practice

Which of the following statements is true of VOX operation versus PTT operation?
It allows "hands free" operation

Generally, who should respond to a station in the contiguous 48 states calling "CQ DX"?
Any stations outside the lower 48 states

What control is typically adjusted for proper ALC setting on a single sideband transceiver?
Transmit audio or microphone gain

Which of the following is true concerning access to frequencies?
Except during emergencies, no amateur station has priority access to any frequency

What is the first thing you should do if you are communicating with another amateur station and hear a station in distress break in?
Acknowledge the station in distress and determine what assistance may be needed

What is good amateur practice if propagation changes during a contact creating interference from other stations using the frequency?
Attempt to resolve the interference problem with the other stations in a mutually acceptable manner

When selecting a CW transmitting frequency, what minimum separation from other stations should be used to minimize interference to stations on adjacent frequencies?
150 Hz to 500 Hz

Take a 15-minute break!!!!!!!!!!!!!!!

Part 2 – Read this section for 45 minutes…

When selecting an SSB transmitting frequency, what minimum separation should be used to minimize interference to stations on adjacent frequencies?
2 kHz to 3 kHz

How can you avoid harmful interference on an apparently clear frequency before calling CQ on CW or phone?
Send "QRL?" on CW, followed by your call sign; or, if using phone, ask if the frequency is in use, followed by your call sign

Which of the following complies with commonly accepted amateur practice when choosing a frequency on which to initiate a call?
Follow the voluntary band plan

What is the voluntary band plan restriction for US stations transmitting within the 48 contiguous states in the 50.1 MHz to 50.125 MHz band segment?
Only contacts with stations not within the 48 contiguous states

Who may be the control operator of an amateur station transmitting in RACES to assist relief operations during a disaster?
Only a person holding an FCC-issued amateur operator license

Which of the following is good amateur practice for net management?
Have a backup frequency in case of interference or poor conditions

How often may RACES training drills and tests be routinely conducted without special authorization?
No more than 1 hour per week

Which of the following describes full break-in CW operation (QSK)?
Transmitting stations can receive between code characters and elements

What should you do if a CW station sends "QRS?"
Send slower

What does it mean when a CW operator sends "KN" at the end of a transmission?
Listening only for a specific station or stations

What does the Q signal "QRL?" mean?
"Are you busy?" or "Is this frequency in use?"

What is the best speed to use when answering a CQ in Morse code?
The fastest speed at which you are comfortable copying, but no faster than the CQ

What does the term "zero beat" mean in CW operation?
Matching the transmit frequency to the frequency of a received signal

When sending CW, what does a "C" mean when added to the RST report?
Chirpy or unstable signal

What prosign is sent to indicate the end of a formal message when using CW?
AR

What does the Q signal "QSL" mean?
I have received and understood

What does the Q signal "QRN" mean?
I am troubled by static

What does the Q signal "QRV" mean?
I am ready to receive

What is the Volunteer Monitor Program?
Amateur volunteers who are formally enlisted to monitor the airwaves for rules violations

Which of the following are objectives of the Volunteer Monitor Program?
To encourage amateur radio operators to self-regulate and comply with the rules

What procedure may be used by Volunteer Monitors to localize a station whose continuous carrier is holding a repeater on in their area?
Compare beam headings on the repeater input from their home locations with that of other Volunteer Monitors

Which of the following describes an azimuthal projection map?
A map that shows true bearings and distances from a specific location

Which of the following indicates that you are looking for an HF contact with any station?
Repeat "CQ" a few times, followed by "this is," then your call sign a few times, then pause to listen, repeat as necessary

How is a directional antenna pointed when making a "long-path" contact with another station?
180 degrees from the station's short-path heading

Which of the following are examples of the NATO Phonetic Alphabet?
Alpha, Bravo, Charlie, Delta

Why do many amateurs keep a station log?
To help with a reply if the FCC requests information about your station

Which of the following is required when participating in a contest on HF frequencies?
Identify your station according to normal FCC regulations

What is QRP operation?
Low-power transmit operation

Why are signal reports typically exchanged at the beginning of an HF contact?
To allow each station to operate according to conditions

Which mode is normally used when sending RTTY signals via AFSK with an SSB transmitter?
LSB

What is VARA?
A digital protocol used with Winlink

What symptoms may result from other signals interfering with a PACTOR or VARA transmission?
Frequent retries or timeouts
Long pauses in message transmission
Failure to establish a connection between stations
All these choices are correct

Which of the following is good practice when choosing a transmitting frequency to answer a station calling CQ using FT8?
Find a clear frequency during the alternate time slot to the calling station

What is the standard sideband for JT65, JT9, FT4, or FT8 digital signal when using AFSK?
USB

What is the most common frequency shift for RTTY emissions in the amateur HF bands?
170 Hz

Which of the following is required when using FT8?
Computer time accurate to within approximately 1 second

In what segment of the 20-meter band are most digital mode operations commonly found?
Between 14.070 MHz and 14.100 MHz

How do you join a contact between two stations using the PACTOR protocol?
Joining an existing contact is not possible, PACTOR connections are limited to two stations

Which of the following is a way to establish contact with a digital messaging system gateway station?
Transmit a connect message on the station's published frequency

What is the primary purpose of an Amateur Radio Emergency Data Network (AREDN) mesh network?
To provide high-speed data services during an emergency or community event

Which of the following describes Winlink?
An amateur radio wireless network to send and receive email on the internet
A form of Packet Radio
A wireless network capable of both VHF and HF band operation
All of the above

What is another name for a Winlink Remote Message Server?
Gateway

What could be wrong if you cannot decode an RTTY or other FSK signal even though it is apparently tuned in properly?
The mark and space frequencies may be reversed
You may have selected the wrong baud rate
You may be listening on the wrong sideband
All these choices are correct

Which of the following is a common location for FT8?
Approximately 14.074 MHz to 14.077 MHz

How does a higher sunspot number affect HF propagation?
Higher sunspot numbers generally indicate a greater probability of good propagation at higher frequencies

What effect does a sudden ionospheric disturbance have on the daytime ionospheric propagation?
It disrupts signals on lower frequencies more than those on higher frequencies

Approximately how long does it take the increased ultraviolet and X-ray radiation from a solar flare to affect radio propagation on Earth?
8 minutes

Which of the following are the least reliable bands for long-distance communications during periods of low solar activity?
15 meters, 12 meters, and 10 meters

What is the solar flux index?
A measure of solar radiation with a wavelength of 10.7 centimeters

What is a geomagnetic storm?
A temporary disturbance in Earth's geomagnetic field

At what point in the solar cycle does the 20-meter band usually support worldwide propagation during daylight hours?
At any point

How can a geomagnetic storm affect HF propagation?
Degrade high-latitude HF propagation

How can high geomagnetic activity benefit radio communications?
Creates auroras that can reflect VHF signals

What causes HF propagation conditions to vary periodically in a 26- to 28-day cycle?
Rotation of the Sun's surface layers around its axis

How long does it take a coronal mass ejection to affect radio propagation on Earth?
15 hours to several days

What does the K-index measure?
The short-term stability of Earth's geomagnetic field

What does the A-index measure?
The long-term stability of Earth's geomagnetic field

How is long distance radio communication usually affected by the charged particles that reach Earth from solar coronal holes?
HF communication is disturbed

What is a characteristic of skywave signals arriving at your location by both short-path and long-path propagation?
A slightly delayed echo might be heard

What factors affect the MUF?
Path distance and location
Time of day and season
Solar radiation and ionospheric disturbances
All these choices are correct

Which frequency will have the least attenuation for long-distance skip propagation?
Just below the MUF

Which of the following is a way to determine current propagation on a desired band from your station?
Use a network of automated receiving stations on the internet to see where your transmissions are being received

How does the ionosphere affect radio waves with frequencies below the MUF and above the LUF?
They are refracted back to Earth

What usually happens to radio waves with frequencies below the LUF?
They are attenuated before reaching the destination

What does LUF stand for?
The Lowest Usable Frequency for communications between two specific points

What does MUF stand for?
The Maximum Usable Frequency for communications between two points

What is the approximate maximum distance along the Earth's surface normally covered in one hop using the F2 region?
2,500 miles

What is the approximate maximum distance along the Earth's surface normally covered in one hop using the E region?
1,200 miles

What happens to HF propagation when the LUF exceeds the MUF?
Propagation via ordinary skywave communications is not possible over that path

Which of the following is typical of the lower HF frequencies during the summer?
High levels of atmospheric noise or static

Which ionospheric region is closest to the surface of Earth?
The D region

What is meant by the term "critical frequency" at a given incidence angle?
The highest frequency which is refracted back to Earth

Why is skip propagation via the F2 region longer than that via the other ionospheric regions?
Because it is the highest

What does the term "critical angle" mean, as applied to radio wave propagation?
The highest takeoff angle that will return a radio wave to Earth under specific ionospheric conditions

Why is long-distance communication on the 40-, 60-, 80-, and 160-meter bands more difficult during the day?
The D region absorbs signals at these frequencies during daylight hours

Take a 15-minute break!!!!!!!!!!!!!!!!!

Part 3 – Read this section for 45 minutes…

What is a characteristic of HF scatter?
Signals have a fluttering sound

What makes HF scatter signals often sound distorted?
Energy is scattered into the skip zone through several different paths

Why are HF scatter signals in the skip zone usually weak?
Only a small part of the signal energy is scattered into the skip zone

What type of propagation allows signals to be heard in the transmitting station's skip zone?
Scatter

What is near vertical incidence skywave (NVIS) propagation?
Short distance MF or HF propagation at high elevation angles

Which ionospheric region is the most absorbent of signals below 10 MHz during daylight hours?
The D region

What is the purpose of the notch filter found on many HF transceivers?
To reduce interference from carriers in the receiver passband

What is the benefit of using the opposite or "reverse" sideband when receiving CW?
It may be possible to reduce or eliminate interference from other signals

How does a noise blanker work?
By reducing receiver gain during a noise pulse

What is the effect on plate current of the correct setting of a vacuum-tube RF power amplifier's TUNE control?
A pronounced dip

Why is automatic level control (ALC) used with an RF power amplifier?
To prevent excessive drive

What is the purpose of an antenna tuner?
Increase power transfer from the transmitter to the feed line

What happens as a receiver's noise reduction control level is increased?
Received signals may become distorted

What is the correct adjustment for the LOAD or COUPLING control of a vacuum tube RF power amplifier?
Desired power output without exceeding maximum allowable plate current

What is the purpose of delaying RF output after activating a transmitter's keying line to an external amplifier?
To allow time for the amplifier to switch the antenna between the transceiver and the amplifier output

What is the function of an electronic keyer?
Automatic generation of dots and dashes for CW operation

Why should the ALC system be inactive when transmitting AFSK data signals?
The ALC action distorts the signal

Which of the following is a common use of the dual-VFO feature on a transceiver?
To transmit on one frequency and listen on another

What is the purpose of using a receive attenuator?
To prevent receiver overload from strong incoming signals

What item of test equipment contains horizontal and vertical channel amplifiers?
An oscilloscope

Which of the following is an advantage of an oscilloscope versus a digital voltmeter?
Complex waveforms can be measured

Which of the following is the best instrument to use for checking the keying waveform of a CW transmitter?
An oscilloscope

What signal source is connected to the vertical input of an oscilloscope when checking the RF envelope pattern of a transmitted signal?
The attenuated RF output of the transmitter

Why do voltmeters have high input impedance?
It decreases the loading on circuits being measured

What is an advantage of a digital multimeter as compared to an analog multimeter?
Higher precision

What signals are used to conduct a two-tone test?
Two non-harmonically related audio signals

What transmitter performance parameter does a two-tone test analyze?
Linearity

When is an analog multimeter preferred to a digital multimeter?
When adjusting circuits for maximum or minimum values

Which of the following can be determined with a directional wattmeter?
Standing wave ratio

Which of the following must be connected to an antenna analyzer when it is being used for SWR measurements?
Antenna and feed line

What effect can strong signals from nearby transmitters have on an antenna analyzer?
Received power that interferes with SWR readings

Which of the following can be measured with an antenna analyzer?
Impedance of coaxial cable

Which of the following might be useful in reducing RF interference to audio frequency circuits?
Bypass capacitor

Which of the following could be a cause of interference covering a wide range of frequencies?
Arcing at a poor electrical connection

What sound is heard from an audio device experiencing RF interference from a single sideband phone transmitter?
Distorted speech

What sound is heard from an audio device experiencing RF interference from a CW transmitter?
On-and-off humming or clicking

What is a possible cause of high voltages that produce RF burns?
The ground wire has high impedance on that frequency

What is a possible effect of a resonant ground connection?
High RF voltages on the enclosures of station equipment

Why should soldered joints not be used in lightning protection ground connections?
A soldered joint will likely be destroyed by the heat of a lightning strike

Which of the following would reduce RF interference caused by common-mode current on an audio cable?
Place a ferrite choke on the cable

How can the effects of ground loops be minimized?
Bond equipment enclosures together

What could be a symptom caused by a ground loop in your station's audio connections?
You receive reports of "hum" on your station's transmitted signal

What technique helps to minimize RF "hot spots" in an amateur station?
Bonding all equipment enclosures together

Why must all metal enclosures of station equipment be grounded?
It ensures that hazardous voltages cannot appear on the chassis

What is the purpose of a speech processor in a transceiver?
Increase the apparent loudness of transmitted voice signals

How does a speech processor affect a single sideband phone signal?
It increases average power

What is the effect of an incorrectly adjusted speech processor?
Distorted speech
Excess intermodulation products
Excessive background noise
All these choices are correct

What does an S meter measure?
Received signal strength

How does a signal that reads 20 dB over S9 compare to one that reads S9 on a receiver, assuming a properly calibrated S meter?
It is 100 times more powerful

How much change in signal strength is typically represented by one S unit?
6 dB

How much must the power output of a transmitter be raised to change the S meter reading on a distant receiver from S8 to S9?
Approximately 4 times

What frequency range is occupied by a 3 kHz LSB signal when the displayed carrier frequency is set to 7.178 MHz?
7.175 MHz to 7.178 MHz

What frequency range is occupied by a 3 kHz USB signal with the displayed carrier frequency set to 14.347 MHz?
14.347 MHz to 14.350 MHz

How close to the lower edge of a band's phone segment should your displayed carrier frequency be when using 3 kHz wide LSB?
At least 3 kHz above the edge of the segment

How close to the upper edge of a band's phone segment should your displayed carrier frequency be when using 3 kHz wide USB?
At least 3 kHz below the edge of the band

What is the purpose of a capacitance hat on a mobile antenna?
To electrically lengthen a physically short antenna

What is the purpose of a corona ball on an HF mobile antenna?
To reduce RF voltage discharge from the tip of the antenna while transmitting

Which of the following direct, fused power connections would be the best for a 100-watt HF mobile installation?
To the battery using heavy-gauge wire

Why should DC power for a 100-watt HF transceiver not be supplied by a vehicle's auxiliary power socket?
The socket's wiring may be inadequate for the current drawn by the transceiver

Which of the following most limits an HF mobile installation?
Efficiency of the electrically short antenna

What is one disadvantage of using a shortened mobile antenna as opposed to a full-size antenna?
Operating bandwidth may be very limited

Which of the following may cause receive interference to an HF transceiver installed in a vehicle?
The battery charging system
The fuel delivery system
The control computers
All these choices are correct

In what configuration are the individual cells in a solar panel connected together?
Series-parallel

What is the approximate open-circuit voltage from a fully illuminated silicon photovoltaic cell?
0.5 VDC

Why should a series diode be connected between a solar panel and a storage battery that is being charged by the panel?
To prevent discharge of the battery through the panel during times of low or no illumination

What precaution should be taken when connecting a solar panel to a lithium iron phosphate battery?
The solar panel must have a charge controller

What happens when inductive and capacitive reactance are equal in a series LC circuit?
Resonance causes impedance to be very low

What is reactance?
Opposition to the flow of alternating current caused by capacitance or inductance

Which of the following is opposition to the flow of alternating current in an inductor?
Reactance

Take a 15-minute break!!!!!!!!!!!!!!!

Part 4 – Read this section for 45 minutes…

Which of the following is opposition to the flow of alternating current in a capacitor?
Reactance

How does an inductor react to AC?
As the frequency of the applied AC increases, the reactance increases

How does a capacitor react to AC?
As the frequency of the applied AC increases, the reactance decreases

What is the term for the inverse of impedance?
Admittance

What is impedance?
The ratio of voltage to current

What unit is used to measure reactance?
Ohm

Which of the following devices can be used for impedance matching at radio frequencies?
A transformer
A Pi-network
A length of transmission line
All these choices are correct

What letter is used to represent reactance?
X

What occurs in an LC circuit at resonance?
Inductive reactance and capacitive reactance cancel

What dB change represents a factor of two increase or decrease in power?
Approximately 3 dB

How does the total current relate to the individual currents in a circuit of parallel resistors?
It equals the sum of the currents through each branch

How many watts of electrical power are consumed if 400 VDC is supplied to an 800-ohm load?
200 watts

How many watts of electrical power are consumed by a 12 VDC light bulb that draws 0.2 amperes?
2.4 watts

How many watts are consumed when a current of 7.0 milliamperes flows through a 1,250-ohm resistance?
Approximately 61 milliwatts

What is the PEP produced by 200 volts peak-to-peak across a 50-ohm dummy load?
100 watts

What value of an AC signal produces the same power dissipation in a resistor as a DC voltage of the same value?
The RMS value

What is the peak-to-peak voltage of a sine wave with an RMS voltage of 120 volts?
339.4 volts

What is the RMS voltage of a sine wave with a value of 17 volts peak?
12 volts

What percentage of power loss is equivalent to a loss of 1 dB?
20.6 percent

What is the ratio of PEP to average power for an unmodulated carrier?
1.00

What is the RMS voltage across a 50-ohm dummy load dissipating 1200 watts?
245 volts

What is the output PEP of an unmodulated carrier if the average power is 1060 watts?
1060 watts

What is the output PEP of 500 volts peak-to-peak across a 50-ohm load?
625 watts

What causes a voltage to appear across the secondary winding of a transformer when an AC voltage source is connected across its primary winding?
Mutual inductance

What is the output voltage if an output signal is applied to the secondary winding of a 4:1 voltage step-down transformer instead of the primary winding?
The input voltage is multiplied by 4

What is the total resistance of a 10-, a 20-, and a 50-ohm resistor connected in parallel?
5.9 ohms

What is the approximate total resistance of a 100- and a 200-ohm resistor in parallel?
67 ohms

Why is the primary winding wire of a voltage step-up transformer usually a larger size than that of the secondary winding?
To accommodate the higher current of the primary

What is the voltage output of a transformer with a 500-turn primary and a 1500-turn secondary when 120 VAC is applied to the primary?
360 volts

What transformer turns ratio matches an antenna's 600-ohm feed point impedance to a 50-ohm coaxial cable?
3.5 to 1

What is the equivalent capacitance of two 5.0-nanofarad capacitors and one 750-picofarad capacitor connected in parallel?
10.750 nanofarads

What is the capacitance of three 100-microfarad capacitors connected in series?
33.3 microfarads

What is the inductance of three 10-millihenry inductors connected in parallel?
3.3 millihenries

What is the inductance of a circuit with a 20-millihenry inductor connected in series with a 50-millihenry inductor?
70 millihenries

What is the capacitance of a 20-microfarad capacitor connected in series with a 50-microfarad capacitor?
14.3 microfarads

Which of the following components should be added to a capacitor to increase the capacitance?
A capacitor in parallel

Which of the following components should be added to an inductor to increase the inductance?
An inductor in series

What is the minimum allowable discharge voltage for maximum life of a standard 12-volt lead-acid battery?
10.5 volts

What is an advantage of batteries with low internal resistance?
High discharge current

What is the approximate forward threshold voltage of a germanium diode?
0.3 volts

Which of the following is characteristic of an electrolytic capacitor?
High capacitance for a given volume

What is the approximate forward threshold voltage of a silicon junction diode?
0.7 volts

Why should wire-wound resistors not be used in RF circuits?
The resistor's inductance could make circuit performance unpredictable

What are the operating points for a bipolar transistor used as a switch?
Saturation and cutoff

Which of the following is characteristic of low voltage ceramic capacitors?
Comparatively low cost

Which of the following describes MOSFET construction?
The gate is separated from the channel by a thin insulating layer

Which element of a vacuum tube regulates the flow of electrons between cathode and plate?
Control grid

What happens when an inductor is operated above its self-resonant frequency?
It becomes capacitive

What is the primary purpose of a screen grid in a vacuum tube?
To reduce grid-to-plate capacitance

What determines the performance of a ferrite core at different frequencies?
The composition, or "mix," of materials used

What is meant by the term MMIC?
Monolithic Microwave Integrated Circuit

Which of the following is an advantage of CMOS integrated circuits compared to TTL integrated circuits?
Low power consumption

What is a typical upper frequency limit for low SWR operation of 50-ohm BNC connectors?
4 GHz

What is an advantage of using a ferrite core toroidal inductor?
Large values of inductance may be obtained
The magnetic properties of the core may be optimized for a specific range of frequencies
Most of the magnetic field is contained in the core
All these choices are correct

What kind of device is an integrated circuit operational amplifier?
Analog

Which of the following describes a type N connector?
A moisture-resistant RF connector useful to 10 GHz

How is an LED biased when emitting light?
Forward biased

How does a ferrite bead or core reduce common-mode RF current on the shield of a coaxial cable?
By creating an impedance in the current's path

What is an SMA connector?
A small threaded connector suitable for signals up to several GHz

Which of these connector types is commonly used for low frequency or dc signal connections to a transceiver?
RCA Phono

What is the function of a power supply bleeder resistor?
It discharges the filter capacitors when power is removed

Which of the following components are used in a power supply filter network?
Capacitors and inductors

Which type of rectifier circuit uses two diodes and a center-tapped transformer?
Full-wave

What is characteristic of a half-wave rectifier in a power supply?
Only one diode is required

What portion of the AC cycle is converted to DC by a half-wave rectifier?
180 degrees

What portion of the AC cycle is converted to DC by a full-wave rectifier?
360 degrees

What is the output waveform of an unfiltered full-wave rectifier connected to a resistive load?
A series of DC pulses at twice the frequency of the AC input

Which of the following is characteristic of a switchmode power supply as compared to a linear power supply?
High-frequency operation allows the use of smaller components

Which symbol in figure G7-1 represents a field effect transistor?
Symbol 1

Which symbol in figure G7-1 represents a Zener diode?
Symbol 5

Which symbol in figure G7-1 represents an NPN junction transistor?
Symbol 2

Which symbol in Figure G7-1 represents a solid core transformer?
Symbol 6

Which symbol in Figure G7-1 represents a tapped inductor?
Symbol 7

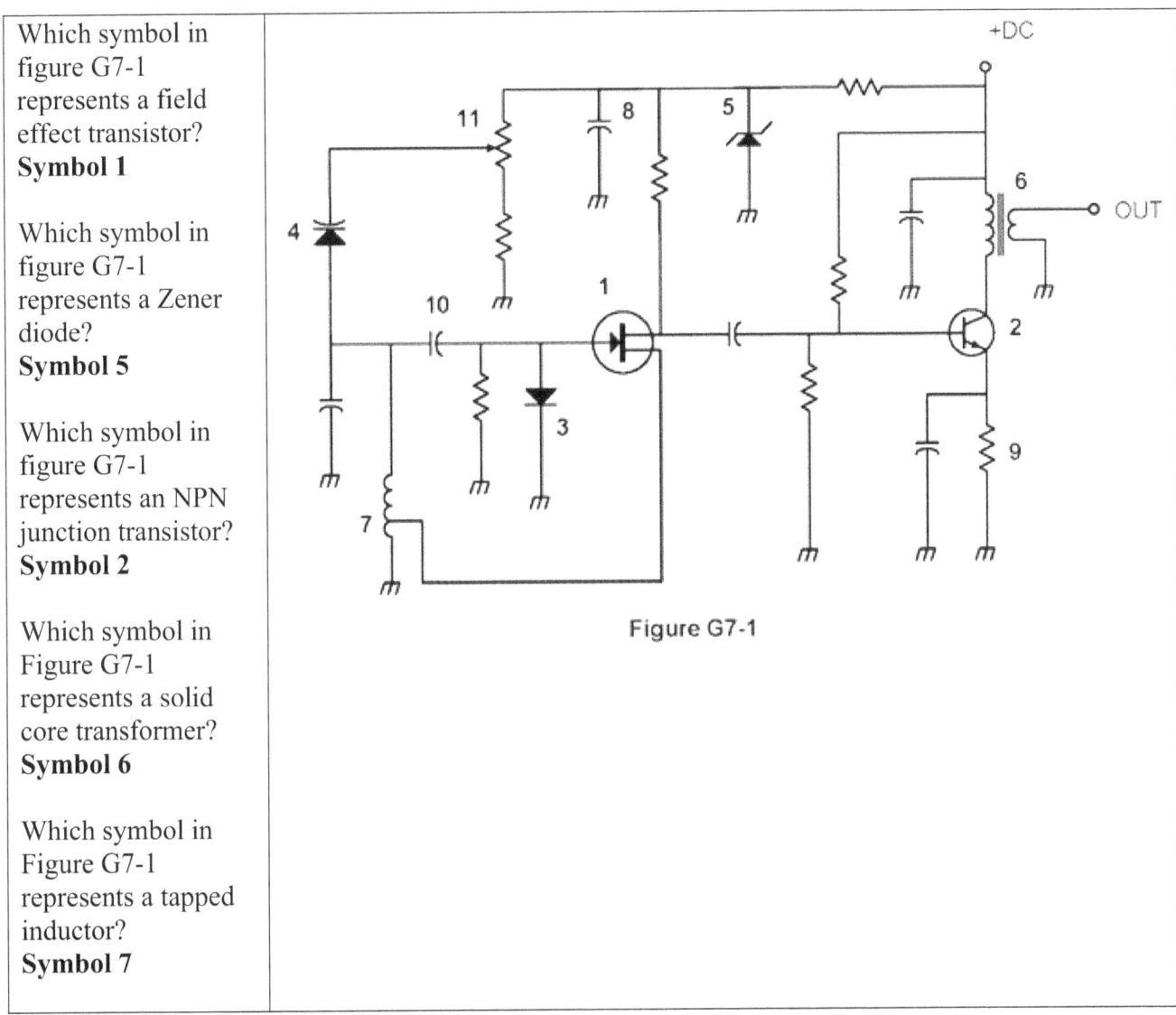

Figure G7-1

What is the purpose of neutralizing an amplifier?
To eliminate self-oscillations

Which of these classes of amplifiers has the highest efficiency?
Class C

Which of the following describes the function of a two-input AND gate?
Output is high only when both inputs are high

In a Class A amplifier, what percentage of the time does the amplifying device conduct?
100%

Take a 15-minute break!!!!!!!!!!!!!!!!

Part 5 – Read this section for 45 minutes…

How many states does a 3-bit binary counter have?
8

What is a shift register?
A clocked array of circuits that passes data in steps along the array

Which of the following are basic components of a sine wave oscillator?
A filter and an amplifier operating in a feedback loop

How is the efficiency of an RF power amplifier determined?
Divide the RF output power by the DC input power

What determines the frequency of an LC oscillator?
The inductance and capacitance in the tank circuit

Which of the following describes a linear amplifier?
An amplifier in which the output preserves the input waveform

For which of the following modes is a Class C power stage appropriate for amplifying a modulated signal?
FM

What circuit is used to select one of the sidebands from a balanced modulator?
Filter

What output is produced by a balanced modulator?
Double-sideband modulated RF

What is one reason to use an impedance matching transformer at a transmitter output?
To present the desired impedance to the transmitter and feed line

How is a product detector used?
Used in a single sideband receiver to extract the modulated signal

Which of the following is characteristic of a direct digital synthesizer (DDS)?
Variable output frequency with the stability of a crystal oscillator

Which of the following is an advantage of a digital signal processing (DSP) filter compared to an analog filter?
A wide range of filter bandwidths and shapes can be created

What term specifies a filter's attenuation inside its passband?
Insertion loss

Which parameter affects receiver sensitivity?
Input amplifier gain
Demodulator stage bandwidth
Input amplifier noise figure
All these choices are correct

What is the phase difference between the I and Q RF signals that software-defined radio (SDR) equipment uses for modulation and demodulation?
90 degrees

What is an advantage of using I-Q modulation with software-defined radios (SDRs)?
All types of modulation can be created with appropriate processing

Which of these functions is performed by software in a software-defined radio (SDR)?
Filtering
Detection
Modulation
All these choices are correct

What is the frequency above which a low-pass filter's output power is less than half the input power?
Cutoff frequency

What term specifies a filter's maximum ability to reject signals outside its passband?
Ultimate rejection

The bandwidth of a band-pass filter is measured between what two frequencies?
Upper and lower half-power

How is direct binary FSK modulation generated?
By changing an oscillator's frequency directly with a digital control signal

What is the name of the process that changes the phase angle of an RF signal to convey information?
Phase modulation

What is the name of the process that changes the instantaneous frequency of an RF wave to convey information?
Frequency modulation

What emission is produced by a reactance modulator connected to a transmitter RF amplifier stage?
Phase modulation

What type of modulation varies the instantaneous power level of the RF signal?
Amplitude modulation

Which of the following is characteristic of QPSK31?
It is sideband sensitive
Its encoding provides error correction
Its bandwidth is approximately the same as BPSK31
All these choices are correct

Which of the following phone emissions uses the narrowest bandwidth?
Single sideband

Which of the following is an effect of overmodulation?
Excessive bandwidth

What type of modulation is used by FT8?
8-tone frequency shift keying

What is meant by the term "flat-topping," when referring to an amplitude-modulated phone signal?
Signal distortion caused by excessive drive or speech levels

What is the modulation envelope of an AM signal?
The waveform created by connecting the peak values of the modulated signal

What is QPSK modulation?
Modulation in which digital data is transmitted using 0-, 90-, 180- and 270-degrees phase shift to represent pairs of bits

What is a link budget?
The sum of transmit power and antenna gains minus system losses as seen at the receiver

What is link margin?
The difference between received power level and minimum required signal level at the input to the receiver

Which mixer input is varied or tuned to convert signals of different frequencies to an intermediate frequency (IF)?
Local oscillator

What is the term for interference from a signal at twice the IF frequency from the desired signal?
Image response

What is another term for the mixing of two RF signals?
Heterodyning

What is the stage in a VHF FM transmitter that generates a harmonic of a lower frequency signal to reach the desired operating frequency?
Multiplier

Which intermodulation products are closest to the original signal frequencies?
Odd-order

What is the total bandwidth of an FM phone transmission having 5 kHz deviation and 3 kHz modulating frequency?
16 kHz

What is the frequency deviation for a 12.21 MHz reactance modulated oscillator in a 5 kHz deviation, 146.52 MHz FM phone transmitter?
416.7 Hz

Why is it important to know the duty cycle of the mode you are using when transmitting?
Some modes have high duty cycles that could exceed the transmitter's average power rating

Why is it good to match receiver bandwidth to the bandwidth of the operating mode?
It results in the best signal-to-noise ratio

What is the relationship between transmitted symbol rate and bandwidth?
Higher symbol rates require wider bandwidth

What combination of a mixer's Local Oscillator (LO) and RF input frequencies is found in the output?
The sum and difference

What process combines two signals in a non-linear circuit to produce unwanted spurious outputs?
Intermodulation

Which of the following is an odd-order intermodulation product of frequencies F1 and F2?
2F1-F2

On what band do amateurs share channels with the unlicensed Wi-Fi service?
2.4 GHz

Which digital mode is used as a low-power beacon for assessing HF propagation?
WSPR

What part of a packet radio frame contains the routing and handling information?
Header

Which of the following describes Baudot code?
A 5-bit code with additional start and stop bits

In an ARQ mode, what is meant by a NAK response to a transmitted packet?
Request retransmission of the packet

What action results from a failure to exchange information due to excessive transmission attempts when using an ARQ mode?
The connection is dropped

Which of the following narrow-band digital modes can receive signals with very low signal-to-noise ratios?
FT8

Which of the following statements is true about PSK31?
Upper case letters use longer Varicode bit sequences and thus slow down transmission

Which is true of mesh network microwave nodes?
If one node fails, a packet may still reach its target station via an alternate node

How does forward error correction (FEC) allow the receiver to correct data errors?
By transmitting redundant information with the data

How are the two separate frequencies of a Frequency Shift Keyed (FSK) signal identified?
Mark and space

Which type of code is used for sending characters in a PSK31 signal?
Varicode

What is indicated on a waterfall display by one or more vertical lines on either side of a data mode or RTTY signal?
Overmodulation

Which of the following describes a waterfall display?
Frequency is horizontal, signal strength is intensity, time is vertical

What does an FT8 signal report of +3 mean?
The signal-to-noise ratio is equivalent to +3dB in a 2.5 kHz bandwidth

Which of the following provide digital voice modes?
DMR, D-STAR, and SystemFusion

Which of the following factors determine the characteristic impedance of a parallel conductor feed line?
The distance between the centers of the conductors and the radius of the conductors

What is the relationship between high standing wave ratio (SWR) and transmission line loss?
High SWR increases loss in a lossy transmission line

Take a 15-minute break!!!!!!!!!!!!!!!

Part 6 – Read this section for 45 minutes…

What is the nominal characteristic impedance of "window line" transmission line?
450 ohms

What causes reflected power at an antenna's feed point?
A difference between feed line impedance and antenna feed point impedance

How does the attenuation of coaxial cable change with increasing frequency?
Attenuation increases

In what units is RF feed line loss usually expressed?
Decibels per 100 feet

What must be done to prevent standing waves on a feed line connected to an antenna?
The antenna feed point impedance must be matched to the characteristic impedance of the feed line

If the SWR on an antenna feed line is 5:1, and a matching network at the transmitter end of the feed line is adjusted to present a 1:1 SWR to the transmitter, what is the resulting SWR on the feed line?
5:1

What standing wave ratio results from connecting a 50-ohm feed line to a 200-ohm resistive load?
4:1

What standing wave ratio results from connecting a 50-ohm feed line to a 10-ohm resistive load?
5:1

What is the effect of transmission line loss on SWR measured at the input to the line?
Higher loss reduces SWR measured at the input to the line

What is a characteristic of a random-wire HF antenna connected directly to the transmitter?
Station equipment may carry significant RF current

Which of the following is a common way to adjust the feed point impedance of an elevated quarter-wave ground-plane vertical antenna to be approximately 50 ohms?
Slope the radials downward

Which of the following best describes the radiation pattern of a quarter-wave ground-plane vertical antenna?
Omnidirectional in azimuth

What is the radiation pattern of a dipole antenna in free space in a plane containing the conductor?
It is a figure-eight at right angles to the antenna

How does antenna height affect the azimuthal radiation pattern of a horizontal dipole HF antenna?
If the antenna is less than 1/2 wavelength high, the azimuthal pattern is almost omnidirectional

Where should the radial wires of a ground-mounted vertical antenna system be placed?
On the surface or buried a few inches below the ground

How does the feed point impedance of a horizontal 1/2 wave dipole antenna change as the antenna height is reduced to 1/10 wavelength above ground?
It steadily decreases

How does the feed point impedance of a 1/2 wave dipole change as the feed point is moved from the center toward the ends?
It steadily increases

Which of the following is an advantage of using a horizontally polarized as compared to a vertically polarized HF antenna?
Lower ground losses

What is the approximate length for a 1/2 wave dipole antenna cut for 14.250 MHz?
33 feet

What is the approximate length for a 1/2 wave dipole antenna cut for 3.550 MHz?
132 feet

What is the approximate length for a 1/4 wave monopole antenna cut for 28.5 MHz?
8 feet

Which of the following would increase the bandwidth of a Yagi antenna?
Larger-diameter elements

What is the approximate length of the driven element of a Yagi antenna?
1/2 wavelength

How do the lengths of a three-element Yagi reflector and director compare to that of the driven element?
The reflector is longer, and the director is shorter

How does antenna gain in dBi compare to gain stated in dBd for the same antenna?
Gain in dBi is 2.15 dB higher

What is the primary effect of increasing boom length and adding directors to a Yagi antenna?
Gain increases

What does "front-to-back ratio" mean in reference to a Yagi antenna?
The power radiated in the major lobe compared to that in the opposite direction

What is meant by the "main lobe" of a directive antenna?
The direction of maximum radiated field strength from the antenna

How does the gain of two three-element, horizontally polarized Yagi antennas spaced vertically 1/2 wavelength apart typically compare to the gain of a single three-element Yagi?
Approximately 3 dB higher

Which of the following can be adjusted to optimize forward gain, front-to-back ratio, or SWR bandwidth of a Yagi antenna?
The physical length of the boom
The number of elements on the boom
The spacing of each element along the boom
All these choices are correct

What is a beta or hairpin match?
A shorted transmission line stub placed at the feed point of a Yagi antenna to provide impedance matching

Which of the following is a characteristic of using a gamma match with a Yagi antenna?
It does not require the driven element to be insulated from the boom

Which of the following antenna types will be most effective as a near vertical incidence skywave (NVIS) antenna for short-skip communications on 40 meters during the day?
A horizontal dipole placed between 1/10 and 1/4 wavelength above the ground

What is the feed point impedance of an end-fed half-wave antenna?
Very high

In which direction is the maximum radiation from a VHF/UHF "halo" antenna?
Omnidirectional in the plane of the halo

What is the primary function of antenna traps?
To enable multiband operation

What is an advantage of vertically stacking horizontally polarized Yagi antennas?
It narrows the main lobe in elevation

Which of the following is an advantage of a log-periodic antenna?
Wide bandwidth

Which of the following describes a log-periodic antenna?
Element length and spacing vary logarithmically along the boom

How does a "screwdriver" mobile antenna adjust its feed point impedance?
By varying the base loading inductance

What is the primary use of a Beverage antenna?
Directional receiving for low HF bands

In which direction or directions does an electrically small loop (less than 1/3 wavelength in circumference) have nulls in its radiation pattern?
Broadside to the loop

Which of the following is a disadvantage of multiband antennas?
They have poor harmonic rejection

What is the common name of a dipole with a single central support?
Inverted V

What is one way that RF energy can affect human body tissue?
It heats body tissue

Which of the following is used to determine RF exposure from a transmitted signal?
Its duty cycle
Its frequency
Its power density
All these choices are correct

How can you determine that your station complies with FCC RF exposure regulations?
By calculation based on FCC OET Bulletin 65
By calculation based on computer modeling
By measurement of field strength using calibrated equipment
All these choices are correct

What does "time averaging" mean when evaluating RF radiation exposure?
The total RF exposure averaged over a certain period

What must you do if an evaluation of your station shows that the RF energy radiated by your station exceeds permissible limits for possible human absorption?
Take action to prevent human exposure to the excessive RF fields

What must you do if your station fails to meet the FCC RF exposure exemption criteria?
Perform an RF Exposure Evaluation in accordance with FCC OET Bulletin 65

What is the effect of modulation duty cycle on RF exposure?
A lower duty cycle permits greater power levels to be transmitted

Which of the following steps must an amateur operator take to ensure compliance with RF safety regulations?
Perform a routine RF exposure evaluation and prevent access to any identified high exposure areas

What type of instrument can be used to accurately measure an RF field strength?
A calibrated field strength meter with a calibrated antenna

What should be done if evaluation shows that a neighbor might experience more than the allowable limit of RF exposure from the main lobe of a directional antenna?
Take precautions to ensure that the antenna cannot be pointed in their direction when they are present

What precaution should be taken if you install an indoor transmitting antenna?
Make sure that MPE limits are not exceeded in occupied areas

What stations are subject to the FCC rules on RF exposure?
All stations with a time-averaged transmission of more than one milliwatt

Which wire or wires in a four-conductor 240 VAC circuit should be attached to fuses or circuit breakers?
Only the hot wires

According to the National Electrical Code, what is the minimum wire size that may be used safely for wiring with a 20-ampere circuit breaker?
AWG number 12

Which size of fuse or circuit breaker would be appropriate to use with a circuit that uses AWG number 14 wiring?
15 amperes

Where should the station's lightning protection ground system be located?
Outside the building

Which of the following conditions will cause a ground fault circuit interrupter (GFCI) to disconnect AC power?
Current flowing from one or more of the hot wires directly to ground

Which of the following is covered by the National Electrical Code?
Electrical safety of the station

Which of these choices should be observed when climbing a tower using a safety harness?
Confirm that the harness is rated for the weight of the climber and that it is within its allowable service life

What should be done before climbing a tower that supports electrically powered devices?
Make sure all circuits that supply power to the tower are locked out and tagged

Which of the following is true of an emergency generator installation?
The generator should be operated in a well-ventilated area

Which of the following is a danger from lead-tin solder?
Lead can contaminate food if hands are not washed carefully after handling the solder

Which of the following is required for lightning protection ground rods?
They must be bonded together with all other grounds

What is the purpose of a power supply interlock?
To ensure that dangerous voltages are removed if the cabinet is opened

Where should lightning arrestors be located?
Where the feed lines enter the building

Ready for Test!!!!!!!!!!!!!!!!

Welcome to the N5HZR Correct Radio Amateur Answers Manual (CRAAM). This manual aims to help you pass the 2024 FCC VE Amateur Radio Element 4, Amateur Extra test. This is not to be confused with a training guide, an operator's guide, or a how-to document. Once you obtain your Amateur Extra license, you'll need to work hard to learn how YOU want to work with radio.

How to use this document:

One way this process works is with the short-term memory we all take for granted. You could plan to take a VE Test some evening and start this process 8 – 10 hours before the test starts. So, let's say the test starts at 6:30 pm. Here's the schedule for the day:

10:00 to 10:45 – Read the **first** segment for 45 minutes.
10:45 to 11:00 – Take a break, hit the restroom, clear your mind.
11:00 to 11:45 – Read the **second** segment for 45 minutes.
11:45 to 12:00 – Take a break, hit the restroom, clear your mind.
12:00 to 12:45 – Read the **third** segment for 45 minutes.
12:45 to 14:00 – Take a break, eat lunch, hit the restroom, clear your mind.
14:00 to 14:45 – Read the **fourth** segment for 45 minutes.
14:45 to 15:00 – Take a break, hit the restroom, clear your mind.
15:00 to 15:45 – Read the **fifth** segment for 45 minutes.
15:45 to 16:00 – Take a break, hit the restroom, clear your mind.
16:00 to 16:45 – Read the **sixth** segment for 45 minutes.
16:45 to 18:30 – Head off to the test site.
18:30 to 19:30 – Relax, take the test.

During each 45-minute reading session, do nothing but rea Turn off all electronic devices. Accept no interruptions. Go somewhere quiet, and away from your normal activities.

The CRAAM guide is laid out with each question listed in normal type, and each CORRECT answer listed in **boldface** text. Don't try to guess the answer. Read and remember each question and answer. This is to plant each CORRECT answer in your short-term memory. You are not trying to understand this information, you're trying to remember this information. There's plenty of time to learn how this works AFTER you get up and running. Take your time... You will have almost 5 minutes to read each page.

Public Domain Release of 2024-2028 Extra Class Question Pool - February 24, 2024 - Effective for VEC Examinations on July 1, 2024, thru June 30, 2028.

Part 1 – Read this section for 45 minutes...

Why is it not legal to transmit a 3 kHz bandwidth USB signal with a carrier frequency of 14.348 MHz?
The upper 1 kHz of the signal is outside the 20-meter band

When using a transceiver that displays the carrier frequency of phone signals, which of the following displayed frequencies represents the lowest frequency at which a properly adjusted LSB emission will be totally within the band?
3 kHz above the lower band edge

What is the highest legal carrier frequency on the 20-meter band for transmitting a 2.8 kHz wide USB data signal?
14.1472 MHz

May an Extra class operator answer the CQ of a station on 3.601 MHz LSB phone?
No, the sideband components will extend beyond the edge of the phone band segment

Who must be in physical control of the station apparatus of an amateur station aboard any vessel or craft that is documented or registered in the United States?
Any person holding an FCC issued amateur license or who is authorized for alien reciprocal operation

What is the required transmit frequency of a CW signal for channelized 60 meter operation?
At the center frequency of the channel

What is the maximum power permitted on the 2200-meter band?
1 watt EIRP (equivalent isotropic radiated power)

If a station in a message forwarding system inadvertently forwards a message that is in violation of FCC rules, who is primarily accountable for the rules violation?
The control operator of the originating station

Except in some parts of Alaska, what is the maximum power permitted on the 630-meter band?
5 watts EIRP (equivalent isotropic radiated power)

If an amateur station is installed aboard a ship or aircraft, what condition must be met before the station is operated?
Its operation must be approved by the master of the ship or the pilot in command of the aircraft

What licensing is required when operating an amateur station aboard a US-registered vessel in international waters?
Any FCC-issued amateur license

Which of the following constitutes a spurious emission?
An emission outside the signal's necessary bandwidth that can be reduced or eliminated without affecting the information transmitted

Which of the following is an acceptable bandwidth for digital voice or slow-scan TV transmissions made on the HF amateur bands?
3 kHz

Within what distance must an amateur station protect an FCC monitoring facility from harmful interference?
1 mile

What must the control operator of a repeater operating in the 70-centimeter band do if a radiolocation system experiences interference from that repeater?
Cease operation or make changes to the repeater that mitigate the interference

What is the National Radio Quiet Zone?
An area surrounding the National Radio Astronomy Observatory

Which of the following additional rules apply if you are erecting an amateur station antenna structure at a site at or near a public use airport?
You may have to notify the Federal Aviation Administration and register it with the FCC as required by Part 17 of the FCC rules

To what type of regulations does PRB-1 apply?
State and local zoning

What limitations may the FCC place on an amateur station if its signal causes interference to domestic broadcast reception, assuming that the receivers involved are of good engineering design?
The amateur station must avoid transmitting during certain hours on frequencies that cause the interference

Which amateur stations may be operated under RACES rules?
Any FCC-licensed amateur station certified by the responsible civil defense organization for the area served

What frequencies are authorized to an amateur station operating under RACES rules?
All amateur service frequencies authorized to the control operator

What does PRB-1 require of state and local regulations affecting amateur radio antenna size and structures?
Reasonable accommodations of amateur radio must be made

What is the maximum bandwidth for a data emission on 60 meters?
2.8 kHz

Which of the following apply to communications transmitted to amateur stations in foreign countries?
Communications must be limited to those incidental to the purpose of the amateur service and remarks of a personal nature

How long must an operator wait after filing a notification with the Utilities Technology Council (UTC) before operating on the 2200-meter or 630-meter band?
Operators may operate after 30 days, providing they have not been told that their station is within 1 kilometer of PLC systems using those frequencies

What is an IARP?
A permit that allows US amateurs to operate in certain countries of the Americas

Under what situation may a station transmit third party communications while being automatically controlled?
Only when transmitting RTTY or data emissions

Which of the following is required in order to operate in accordance with CEPT rules in foreign countries where permitted?
You must have a copy of FCC Public Notice DA 16-1048

What notifications must be given before transmitting on the 630- or 2200-meter bands?
Operators must inform the Utilities Technology Council (UTC) of their call sign and coordinates of the station

What is the maximum permissible duration of a remotely controlled station's transmissions if its control link malfunctions?
3 minutes

What is the highest modulation index permitted at the highest modulation frequency for angle modulation below 29.0 MHz?
1.0

What is the maximum mean power level for a spurious emission below 30 MHz with respect to the fundamental emission?
- 43 dB

Which of the following operating arrangements allows an FCC-licensed US citizen to operate in many European countries, and amateurs from many European countries to operate in the US?
CEPT

In what portion of the 630-meter band are phone emissions permitted?
The entire band

What is the definition of telemetry?
One-way transmission of measurements at a distance from the measuring instrument

Which of the following may transmit encrypted messages?
Telecommand signals from a space telecommand station

What is a space telecommand station?
An amateur station that transmits communications to initiate, modify, or terminate functions of a space station

Which of the following is required in the identification transmissions from a balloon-borne telemetry station?
Call sign

What must be posted at the location of a station being operated by telecommand on or within 50 kilometers of the Earth's surface?
A photocopy of the station license
A label with the name, address, and telephone number of the station licensee
A label with the name, address, and telephone number of the control operator
All these choices are correct

What is the maximum permitted transmitter output power when operating a model craft by telecommand?
1 watt

Which of the following HF amateur bands include allocations for space stations?
40 meters, 20 meters, 15 meters, and 10 meters

Which VHF amateur bands have frequencies authorized for space stations?
2 meters

Which UHF amateur bands have frequencies authorized for space stations?
70 centimeters and 13 centimeters

Which amateur stations are eligible to be telecommand stations of space stations, subject to the privileges of the class of operator license held by the control operator of the station?
Any amateur station so designated by the space station licensee

Which amateur stations are eligible to operate as Earth stations?
Any amateur station, subject to the privileges of the class of operator license held by the control operator

Which of the following amateur stations may transmit one-way communications?
A space station, beacon station, or telecommand station

For which types of out-of-pocket expenses do the Part 97 rules state that VEs and VECs may be reimbursed?
Preparing, processing, administering, and coordinating an examination for an amateur radio operator license

Who is tasked by Part 97 with maintaining the pools of questions for all US amateur license examinations?
The VECs

What is a Volunteer Examiner Coordinator?
An organization that has entered into an agreement with the FCC to coordinate, prepare, and administer amateur operator license examinations

What is required to be accredited as a Volunteer Examiner?
A VEC must confirm that the VE applicant meets FCC requirements to serve as an examiner

What must the VE team do with the application form if the examinee does not pass the exam?
Return the application document to the examinee

Who is responsible for the proper conduct and necessary supervision during an amateur operator license examination session?
Each administering VE

What should a VE do if a candidate fails to comply with the examiner's instructions during an amateur operator license examination?
Immediately terminate the candidate's examination

To which of the following examinees may a VE not administer an examination?
Relatives of the VE as listed in the FCC rules

What may be the penalty for a VE who fraudulently administers or certifies an examination?
Revocation of the VE's amateur station license grant and the suspension of the VE's amateur operator license grant

What must the administering VEs do after the administration of a successful examination for an amateur operator license?
They must submit the application document to the coordinating VEC according to the coordinating VEC instructions

What must the VE team do if an examinee scores a passing grade on all examination elements needed for an upgrade or new license?
Three VEs must certify that the examinee is qualified for the license grant and that they have complied with the administering VE requirements

On what frequencies are spread spectrum transmissions permitted?
Only on amateur frequencies above 222 MHz

What privileges are authorized in the US to persons holding an amateur service license granted by the government of Canada?
The operating terms and conditions of the Canadian amateur service license, not to exceed US Amateur Extra class license privileges

Under what circumstances may a dealer sell an external RF power amplifier capable of operation below 144 MHz if it has not been granted FCC certification?
The amplifier is constructed or modified by an amateur radio operator for use at an amateur station

Which of the following geographic descriptions approximately describes "Line A"?
A line roughly parallel to and south of the border between the US and Canada

Amateur stations may not transmit in which of the following frequency segments if they are located in the contiguous 48 states and north of Line A?
420 MHz - 430 MHz

Under what circumstances might the FCC issue a Special Temporary Authority (STA) to an amateur station?
To provide for experimental amateur communications

When may an amateur station send a message to a business?
When neither the amateur nor their employer has a pecuniary interest in the communications

Which of the following types of amateur station communications are prohibited?
Communications transmitted for hire or material compensation, except as otherwise provided in the rules

Which of the following cannot be transmitted over an amateur radio mesh network?
Messages encoded to obscure their meaning

Who may be the control operator of an auxiliary station?
Only Technician, General, Advanced, or Amateur Extra class operators

Which of the following best describes one of the standards that must be met by an external RF power amplifier if it is to qualify for a grant of FCC certification?
It must satisfy the FCC's spurious emission standards when operated at the lesser of 1500 watts or its full output power

What is the direction of an ascending pass for an amateur satellite?
From south to north

Which of the following is characteristic of an inverting linear transponder?
Doppler shift is reduced because the uplink and downlink shifts are in opposite directions
Signal position in the band is reversed
Upper sideband on the uplink becomes lower sideband on the downlink, and vice versa
All these choices are correct

How is an upload signal processed by an inverting linear transponder?
The signal is mixed with a local oscillator signal and the difference product is transmitted

What is meant by the "mode" of an amateur radio satellite?
The satellite's uplink and downlink frequency bands

What do the letters in a satellite's mode designator specify?
The uplink and downlink frequency ranges

What are Keplerian elements?
Parameters that define the orbit of a satellite

Which of the following types of signals can be relayed through a linear transponder?
FM and CW
SSB and SSTV
PSK and packet
All these choices are correct

Why should effective radiated power (ERP) be limited to a satellite that uses a linear transponder?
To avoid reducing the downlink power to all other users

What do the terms "L band" and "S band" specify?
The 23- and 13-centimeter bands

What type of satellite appears to stay in one position in the sky?
Geostationary

What type of antenna can be used to minimize the effects of spin modulation and Faraday rotation?
A circularly polarized antenna

What is the purpose of digital store-and-forward functions on an amateur radio satellite?
To hold digital messages in the satellite for later download

Which of the following techniques is used by digital satellites to relay messages?
Store-and-forward

In digital television, what does a coding rate of 3/4 mean?
25% of the data sent is forward error correction data

How many horizontal lines make up a fast-scan (NTSC) television frame?
525

How is an interlaced scanning pattern generated in a fast-scan (NTSC) television system?
By scanning odd-numbered lines in one field and even-numbered lines in the next

How is color information sent in analog SSTV?
Color lines are sent sequentially

Which of the following describes the use of vestigial sideband in analog fast-scan TV transmissions?
Vestigial sideband reduces the bandwidth while increasing the fidelity of low frequency video components

What is vestigial sideband modulation?
Amplitude modulation in which one complete sideband and a portion of the other are transmitted

Which types of modulation are used for amateur television DVB-T signals?
QAM and QPSK

What technique allows commercial analog TV receivers to be used for fast-scan TV operations on the 70-centimeter band?
Transmitting on channels shared with cable TV

What kind of receiver can be used to receive and decode SSTV using the Digital Radio Mondiale (DRM) protocol?
SSB

What aspect of an analog slow-scan television signal encodes the brightness of the picture?
Tone frequency

What is the function of the vertical interval signaling (VIS) code sent as part of an SSTV transmission?
To identify the SSTV mode being used

What signals SSTV receiving software to begin a new picture line?
Specific tone frequencies

End of Section 1. Rest a bit, relax, and start again when ready.

Part 2 – Read this section for 45 minutes...

What indicator is required to be used by US-licensed operators when operating a station via remote control and the remote transmitter is located in the US?
No additional indicator is required

Which of the following file formats is used for exchanging amateur radio log data?
ADIF

From which of the following bands is amateur radio contesting generally excluded?
30 meters

Which of the following frequencies can be used for amateur radio mesh networks?
Frequencies shared with various unlicensed wireless data services

What is the function of a DX QSL Manager?
Handle the receiving and sending of confirmations for a DX station

During a VHF/UHF contest, in which band segment would you expect to find the highest level of SSB or CW activity?
In the weak signal segment of the band, with most of the activity near the calling frequency

What is the Cabrillo format?
A standard for submission of electronic contest logs

Which of the following contacts may be confirmed through the Logbook of The World (LoTW)?
Special event contacts between stations in the US
Contacts between a US station and a non-US station
Contacts for Worked All States credit
All these choices are correct

What type of equipment is commonly used to implement an amateur radio mesh network?
A wireless router running custom firmware

Why do DX stations often transmit and receive on different frequencies?
Because the DX station may be transmitting on a frequency that is prohibited to some responding stations
To separate the calling stations from the DX station
To improve operating efficiency by reducing interference
All these choices are correct

How should you generally identify your station when attempting to contact a DX station during a contest or in a pileup?
Send your full call sign once or twice

What indicates the delay between a control operator action and the corresponding change in the transmitted signal?
Latency

Which of the following digital modes is designed for meteor scatter communications?
MSK144

What information replaces signal-to-noise ratio when using the FT8 or FT4 modes in a VHF contest?
Grid square

Which of the following digital modes is designed for EME communications?
Q65

What technology is used for real-time tracking of balloons carrying amateur radio transmitters?
APRS

What is the characteristic of the JT65 mode?
Decodes signals with a very low signal-to-noise ratio

Which of the following is a method for establishing EME contacts?
Time-synchronous transmissions alternating between stations

What digital protocol is used by APRS?
AX.25

What type of packet frame is used to transmit APRS beacon data?
Unnumbered Information

What type of modulation is used by JT65?
Multitone AFSK

What does the packet path WIDE3-1 designate?
Three digipeater hops are requested with one remaining

How do APRS stations relay data?
By packet digipeaters

Which of the following types of modulation is used for data emissions below 30 MHz?
FSK

Which of the following synchronizes WSJT-X digital mode transmit/receive timing?
Synchronization of computer clocks

To what does the "4" in FT4 refer?
Four-tone continuous-phase frequency shift keying

Which of the following is characteristic of the FST4 mode?
Four-tone Gaussian frequency shift keying
Variable transmit/receive periods
Seven different tone spacings
All these choices are correct

Which of these digital modes does not support keyboard-to-keyboard operation?
WSPR

What is the length of an FT8 transmission cycle?
15 seconds

How does Q65 differ from JT65?
Multiple receive cycles are averaged

Which of the following HF digital modes can be used to transfer binary files?
PACTOR

Which of the following HF digital modes uses variable-length character coding?
PSK31

Which of these digital modes has the narrowest bandwidth?
FT8

What is the difference between direct FSK and audio FSK?
Direct FSK modulates the transmitter VFO

How do ALE stations establish contact?
ALE constantly scans a list of frequencies, activating the radio when the designated call sign is received

Which of these digital modes has the highest data throughput under clear communication conditions?
PACTOR IV

What is the approximate maximum separation measured along the surface of the Earth between two stations communicating by EME?
12,000 miles, if the moon is "visible" by both stations

What characterizes libration fading of an EME signal?
A fluttery, irregular fading

When scheduling EME contacts, which of these conditions will generally result in the least path loss?
When the Moon is at perigee

In what direction does an electromagnetic wave travel?
It travels at a right angle to the electric and magnetic fields

How are the component fields of an electromagnetic wave oriented?
They are at right angles

What should be done to continue a long-distance contact when the MUF for that path decreases due to darkness?
Switch to a lower frequency HF band

Atmospheric ducts capable of propagating microwave signals often form over what geographic feature?
Large bodies of water

When a meteor strikes the Earth's atmosphere, a linear ionized region is formed at what region of the ionosphere?
The E region

Which of the following frequency ranges is most suited for meteor-scatter communications?
28 MHz - 148 MHz

What determines the speed of electromagnetic waves through a medium?
The index of refraction

What is a typical range for tropospheric duct propagation of microwave signals?
100 miles to 300 miles

What is most likely to result in auroral propagation?
Severe geomagnetic storms

Which of these emission modes is best for auroral propagation?
CW

What are circularly polarized electromagnetic waves?
Waves with rotating electric and magnetic fields

Where is transequatorial propagation (TEP) most likely to occur?
Between points separated by 2,000 miles to 3,000 miles over a path perpendicular to the geomagnetic equator

What is the approximate maximum range for signals using transequatorial propagation?
5,000 miles

At what time of day is transequatorial propagation most likely to occur?
Afternoon or early evening

What are "extraordinary" and "ordinary" waves?
Independently propagating, elliptically polarized waves created in the ionosphere

Which of the following paths is most likely to support long-distance propagation on 160 meters?
A path entirely in darkness

On which of the following amateur bands is long-path propagation most frequent?
40 meters and 20 meters

What effect does lowering a signal's transmitted elevation angle have on ionospheric HF skip propagation?
The distance covered by each hop increases

How does the maximum range of ground-wave propagation change when the signal frequency is increased?
It decreases

At what time of year is sporadic-E propagation most likely to occur?
Around the solstices, especially the summer solstice

What is the effect of chordal-hop propagation?
The signal experiences less loss compared to multi-hop propagation, which uses Earth as a reflector

At what time of day is sporadic-E propagation most likely to occur?
Between sunrise and sunset

What is chordal-hop propagation?
Successive ionospheric refractions without an intermediate reflection from the ground

What type of polarization is supported by ground-wave propagation?
Vertical

What is the cause of short-term radio blackouts?
Solar flares

What is indicated by a rising A-index or K-index?
Increasing disturbance of the geomagnetic field

Which of the following signal paths is most likely to experience high levels of absorption when the A-index or K-index is elevated?
Through the auroral oval

What does the value of Bz (B sub z) represent?
North-south strength of the interplanetary magnetic field

What orientation of Bz (B sub z) increases the likelihood that charged particles from the Sun will cause disturbed conditions?
Southward

How does the VHF/UHF radio horizon compare to the geographic horizon?
It is approximately 15 percent farther

Which of the following indicates the greatest solar flare intensity?
Class X

Which of the following is the space-weather term for an extreme geomagnetic storm?
G5

What type of data is reported by amateur radio propagation reporting networks?
Digital-mode and CW signals

What does the 304A solar parameter measure?
UV emissions at 304 angstroms, correlated to the solar flux index

What does VOACAP software model?
HF propagation

Which of the following is indicated by a sudden rise in radio background noise across a large portion of the HF spectrum?
A coronal mass ejection impact or a solar flare has occurred

Which of the following limits the highest frequency signal that can be accurately displayed on a digital oscilloscope?
Sampling rate of the analog-to-digital converter

Which of the following parameters does a spectrum analyzer display on the vertical and horizontal axes?
Signal amplitude and frequency

Which of the following test instruments is used to display spurious signals and/or intermodulation distortion products generated by an SSB transmitter?
Spectrum analyzer

How is compensation of an oscilloscope probe performed?
A square wave is displayed, and the probe is adjusted until the horizontal portions of the displayed wave are as nearly flat as possible

What is the purpose of using a prescaler with a frequency counter?
Reduce the signal frequency to within the counter's operating range

What is the effect of aliasing on a digital oscilloscope when displaying a waveform?
A false, jittery low-frequency version of the waveform is displayed

Which of the following is an advantage of using an antenna analyzer compared to an SWR bridge?
Antenna analyzers compute SWR and impedance automatically

Which of the following is used to measure SWR?
Directional wattmeter
Vector network analyzer
Antenna analyzer
All these choices are correct

Which of the following is good practice when using an oscilloscope probe?
Minimize the length of the probe's ground connection

Which trigger mode is most effective when using an oscilloscope to measure a linear power supply's output ripple?
Line

Which of the following can be measured with an antenna analyzer?
Velocity factor
Cable length
Resonant frequency of a tuned circuit
All these choices are correct

Which of the following factors most affects the accuracy of a frequency counter?
Time base accuracy

What is the significance of voltmeter sensitivity expressed in ohms per volt?
The full scale reading of the voltmeter multiplied by its ohms per volt rating is the input impedance of the voltmeter

Which S parameter is equivalent to forward gain?
S21

Which S parameter represents input port return loss or reflection coefficient (equivalent to VSWR)?
S11

What three test loads are used to calibrate an RF vector network analyzer?
Short circuit, open circuit, and 50 ohms

How much power is being absorbed by the load when a directional power meter connected between a transmitter and a terminating load reads 100 watts forward power and 25 watts reflected power?
75 watts

What do the subscripts of S parameters represent?
The port or ports at which measurements are made

Which of the following can be used to determine the Q of a series-tuned circuit?
The bandwidth of the circuit's frequency response

Which of the following can be measured by a two-port vector network analyzer?
Filter frequency response

Which of the following methods measures intermodulation distortion in an SSB transmitter?
Modulate the transmitter using two AF signals having non-harmonically related frequencies and observe the RF output with a spectrum analyzer

Which of the following can be measured with a vector network analyzer?
Input impedance
Output impedance
Reflection coefficient
All these choices are correct

What is an effect of excessive phase noise in an SDR receiver's master clock oscillator?
It can combine with strong signals on nearby frequencies to generate interference

Which of the following receiver circuits can be effective in eliminating interference from strong out-of-band signals?
A front-end filter or preselector

What is the term for the suppression in an FM receiver of one signal by another stronger signal on the same frequency?
Capture effect

What is the noise figure of a receiver?
The ratio in dB of the noise generated by the receiver to the theoretical minimum noise

End of Section 2. Rest a bit, relax, and start again when ready.

Part 3 – Read this section for 45 minutes...

What does a receiver noise floor of -174 dBm represent?
The theoretical noise in a 1 Hz bandwidth at the input of a perfect receiver at room temperature

How much does increasing a receiver's bandwidth from 50 Hz to 1,000 Hz increase the receiver's noise floor?
13 dB

What does the MDS of a receiver represent?
The minimum discernible signal

An SDR receiver is overloaded when input signals exceed what level?
The reference voltage of the analog-to-digital converter

Which of the following choices is a good reason for selecting a high IF for a superheterodyne HF or VHF communications receiver?
Easier for front-end circuitry to eliminate image responses

What is an advantage of having a variety of receiver bandwidths from which to select?
Receive bandwidth can be set to match the modulation bandwidth, maximizing signal-to-noise ratio and minimizing interference

Why does input attenuation reduce receiver overload on the lower frequency HF bands with little or no impact on signal-to-noise ratio?
Atmospheric noise is generally greater than internally generated noise even after attenuation

How does a narrow-band roofing filter affect receiver performance?
It improves blocking dynamic range by attenuating strong signals near the receive frequency

What is reciprocal mixing?
Local oscillator phase noise mixing with adjacent strong signals to create interference to desired signals

What is the purpose of the receiver IF Shift control?
To reduce interference from stations transmitting on adjacent frequencies

What is meant by the blocking dynamic range of a receiver?
The difference in dB between the noise floor and the level of an incoming signal that will cause 1 dB of gain compression

Which of the following describes problems caused by poor dynamic range in a receiver?
Spurious signals caused by cross modulation and desensitization from strong adjacent signals

What creates intermodulation interference between two repeaters in close proximity?
The output signals mix in the final amplifier of one or both transmitters

Which of the following is used to reduce or eliminate intermodulation interference in a repeater caused by a nearby transmitter?
A properly terminated circulator at the output of the repeater's transmitter

What transmitter frequencies would create an intermodulation-product signal in a receiver tuned to 146.70 MHz when a nearby station transmits on 146.52 MHz?
146.34 MHz and 146.61 MHz

What is the term for the reduction in receiver sensitivity caused by a strong signal near the received frequency?
Desensitization

Which of the following reduces the likelihood of receiver desensitization?
Insert attenuation before the first RF stage

What causes intermodulation in an electronic circuit?
Nonlinear circuits or devices

What is the purpose of the preselector in a communications receiver?
To increase the rejection of signals outside the band being received

What does a third-order intercept level of 40 dBm mean with respect to receiver performance?
A pair of 40 dBm input signals will theoretically generate a third-order intermodulation product that has the same output amplitude as either of the input signals

Why are odd-order intermodulation products, created within a receiver, of particular interest compared to other products?
Odd-order products of two signals in the band being received are also likely to be within the band

What is the link margin in a system with a transmit power level of 10 W (+40 dBm), a system antenna gain of 10 dBi, a cable loss of 3 dB, a path loss of 136 dB, a receiver minimum discernable signal of -103 dBm, and a required signal-to-noise ratio of 6 dB?
+8dB

What is the received signal level with a transmit power of 10 W (+40 dBm), a transmit antenna gain of 6 dBi, a receive antenna gain of 3 dBi, and a path loss of 100 dB?
-51 dBm

What power level does a receiver minimum discernible signal of -100 dBm represent?
0.1 picowatts

What problem can occur when using an automatic notch filter (ANF) to remove interfering carriers while receiving CW signals?
Removal of the CW signal as well as the interfering carrier

Which of the following types of noise can often be reduced by a digital noise reduction?
Broadband white noise
Ignition noise
Power line noise
All these choices are correct

Which of the following types of noise are removed by a noise blanker?
Impulse noise

How can conducted noise from an automobile battery charging system be suppressed?
By installing ferrite chokes on the charging system leads

What is used to suppress radio frequency interference from a line-driven AC motor?
A brute-force AC-line filter in series with the motor's power leads

What type of electrical interference can be caused by computer network equipment?
The appearance of unstable modulated or unmodulated signals at specific frequencies

Which of the following can cause shielded cables to radiate or receive interference?
Common-mode currents on the shield and conductors

What current flows equally on all conductors of an unshielded multiconductor cable?
Common-mode current

What undesirable effect can occur when using a noise blanker?
Strong signals may be distorted and appear to cause spurious emissions

Which of the following can create intermittent loud roaring or buzzing AC line interference?
Arcing contacts in a thermostatically controlled device
A defective doorbell or doorbell transformer inside a nearby residence
A malfunctioning illuminated advertising display
All these choices are correct

What could be the cause of local AM broadcast band signals combining to generate spurious signals on the MF or HF bands?
Nearby corroded metal connections are mixing and reradiating the broadcast signals

What causes interference received as a series of carriers at regular intervals across a wide frequency range?
Switch-mode power supplies

Where should a station AC surge protector be installed?
On the single point ground panel

What is the purpose of a single point ground panel?
Ensure all lightning protectors activate at the same time

What can cause the voltage across reactances in a series RLC circuit to be higher than the voltage applied to the entire circuit?
Resonance

What is the resonant frequency of an RLC circuit if R is 22 ohms, L is 50 microhenries, and C is 40 picofarads?
3.56 MHz

What is the magnitude of the impedance of a series RLC circuit at resonance?
Approximately equal to circuit resistance

What is the magnitude of the impedance of a parallel RLC circuit at resonance?
Approximately equal to circuit resistance

What is the result of increasing the Q of an impedance-matching circuit?
Matching bandwidth is decreased

What is the magnitude of the circulating current within the components of a parallel LC circuit at resonance?
It is at a maximum

What is the magnitude of the current at the input of a parallel RLC circuit at resonance?
Minimum

What is the phase relationship between the current through and the voltage across a series resonant circuit at resonance?
The voltage and current are in phase

How is the Q of an RLC parallel resonant circuit calculated?
Resistance divided by the reactance of either the inductance or capacitance

What is the resonant frequency of an RLC circuit if R is 33 ohms, L is 50 microhenries, and C is 10 picofarads?
7.12 MHz

What is the half-power bandwidth of a resonant circuit that has a resonant frequency of 7.1 MHz and a Q of 150?
47.3 kHz

What is the half-power bandwidth of a resonant circuit that has a resonant frequency of 3.7 MHz and a Q of 118?
31.4 kHz

What is an effect of increasing Q in a series resonant circuit?
Internal voltages increase

What is the term for the time required for the capacitor in an RC circuit to be charged to 63.2% of the applied voltage or to discharge to 36.8% of its initial voltage?
One time constant

What letter is commonly used to represent susceptance?
B

How is impedance in polar form converted to an equivalent admittance?
Take the reciprocal of the magnitude and change the sign of the angle

What is the time constant of a circuit having two 220-microfarad capacitors and two 1-megohm resistors, all in parallel?
220 seconds

What is the effect on the magnitude of pure reactance when it is converted to susceptance?
It is replaced by its reciprocal

What is susceptance?
The imaginary part of admittance

What is the phase angle between the voltage across and the current through a series RLC circuit if XC is 500 ohms, R is 1 kilohm, and XL is 250 ohms?
14.0 degrees with the voltage lagging the current

What is the phase angle between the voltage across and the current through a series RLC circuit if XC is 300 ohms, R is 100 ohms, and XL is 100 ohms?
63 degrees with the voltage lagging the current

What is the relationship between the AC current through a capacitor and the voltage across a capacitor?
Current leads voltage by 90 degrees

What is the relationship between the AC current through an inductor and the voltage across an inductor?
Voltage leads current by 90 degrees

What is the phase angle between the voltage across and the current through a series RLC circuit if XC is 25 ohms, R is 100 ohms, and XL is 75 ohms?
27 degrees with the voltage leading the current

What is admittance?
The inverse of impedance

Which of the following represents pure capacitive reactance of 100 ohms in rectangular notation?
0 - j100

How are impedances described in polar coordinates?
By magnitude and phase angle

Which of the following represents a pure inductive reactance in polar coordinates?
A positive 90 degree phase angle

What type of Y-axis scale is most often used for graphs of circuit frequency response?
Logarithmic

What kind of diagram is used to show the phase relationship between impedances at a given frequency?
Phasor diagram

What does the impedance 50 - j25 ohms represent?
50 ohms resistance in series with 25 ohms capacitive reactance

Where is the impedance of a pure resistance plotted on rectangular coordinates?
On the horizontal axis

What coordinate system is often used to display the phase angle of a circuit containing resistance, inductive, and/or capacitive reactance?
Polar coordinates

When using rectangular coordinates to graph the impedance of a circuit, what do the axes represent?
The X axis represents the resistive component, and the Y axis represents the reactive component

Which point on Figure E5-1 best represents the impedance of a series circuit consisting of a 400-ohm resistor and a 38-picofarad capacitor at 14 MHz?
Point 4

Which point in Figure E5-1 best represents the impedance of a series circuit consisting of a 300-ohm resistor and an 18-microhenry inductor at 3.505 MHz?
Point 3

Which point on Figure E5-1 best represents the impedance of a series circuit consisting of a 300-ohm resistor and a 19-picofarad capacitor at 21.200 MHz?
Point 1

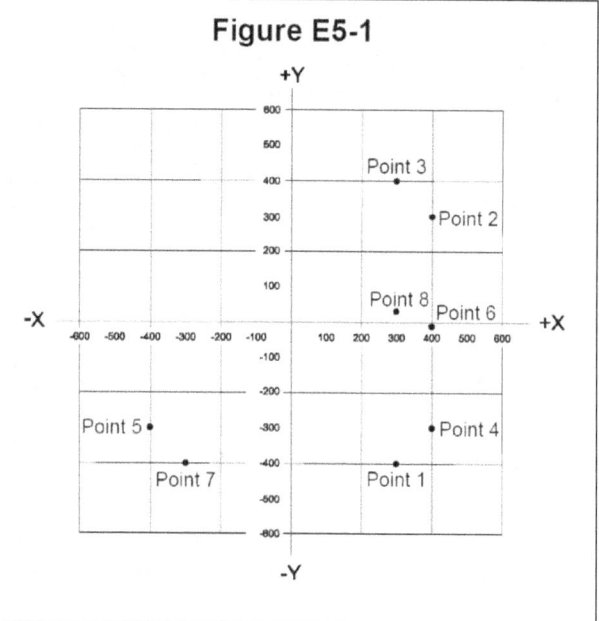

Figure E5-1

What is the result of conductor skin effect?
Resistance increases as frequency increases because RF current flows closer to the surface

Why is it important to keep lead lengths short for components used in circuits for VHF and above?
To minimize inductive reactance

What is the phase relationship between current and voltage for reactive power?
They are 90 degrees out of phase

Why are short connections used at microwave frequencies?
To reduce phase shift along the connection

What parasitic characteristic causes electrolytic capacitors to be unsuitable for use at RF?
Inductance

What parasitic characteristic creates an inductor's self-resonance?
Inter-turn capacitance

What combines to create the self-resonance of a component?
The component's nominal and parasitic reactance

What is the primary cause of loss in film capacitors at RF?
Skin effect

What happens to reactive power in ideal inductors and capacitors?
Energy is stored in magnetic or electric fields, but power is not dissipated

As a conductor's diameter increases, what is the effect on its electrical length?
It increases

How much real power is consumed in a circuit consisting of a 100-ohm resistor in series with a 100-ohm inductive reactance drawing 1 ampere?
100 watts

What is reactive power?
Wattless, nonproductive power

In what application is gallium arsenide used as a semiconductor material?
In microwave circuits

Which of the following semiconductor materials contains excess free electrons?
N-type

Why does a PN-junction diode not conduct current when reverse biased?
Holes in P-type material and electrons in the N-type material are separated by the applied voltage, widening the depletion region

What is the name given to an impurity atom that adds holes to a semiconductor crystal structure?
Acceptor impurity

How does DC input impedance at the gate of a field-effect transistor (FET) compare with that of a bipolar transistor?
An FET has higher input impedance

What is the beta of a bipolar junction transistor?
The change in collector current with respect to the change in base current

Which of the following indicates that a silicon NPN junction transistor is biased on?
Base-to-emitter voltage of approximately 0.6 volts to 0.7 volts

What is the term for the frequency at which the grounded-base current gain of a bipolar junction transistor has decreased to 0.7 of the gain obtainable at 1 kHz?
Alpha cutoff frequency

What is a depletion-mode field-effect transistor (FET)?
An FET that exhibits a current flow between source and drain when no gate voltage is applied

End of Section 3. Rest a bit, relax, and start again when ready.

Part 4 – Read this section for 45 minutes...

In Figure E6-1, which is the schematic symbol for an N-channel dual-gate MOSFET? **4** In Figure E6-1, which is the schematic symbol for a P-channel junction FET? **1**	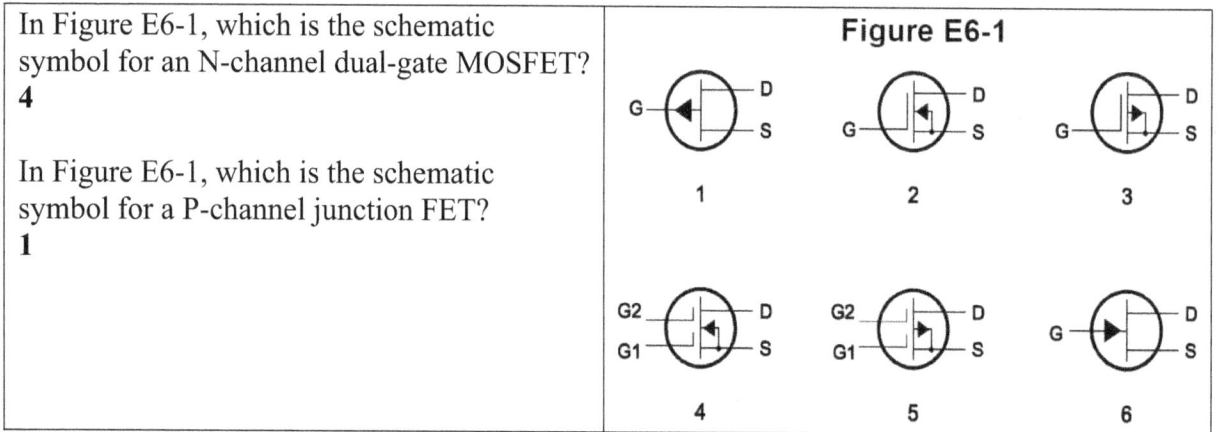

What is the purpose of connecting Zener diodes between a MOSFET gate and its source or drain?
To protect the gate from static damage

What is the most useful characteristic of a Zener diode?
A constant voltage drop under conditions of varying current

Which characteristic of a Schottky diode makes it a better choice than a silicon junction diode for use as a power supply rectifier?
Lower forward voltage drop

What property of an LED's semiconductor material determines its forward voltage drop?
Band gap

What type of semiconductor device is designed for use as a voltage-controlled capacitor?
Varactor diode

What characteristic of a PIN diode makes it useful as an RF switch?
Low junction capacitance

Which of the following is a common use of a Schottky diode?
As a VHF/UHF mixer or detector

What causes a junction diode to fail from excessive current?
Excessive junction temperature

Which of the following is a Schottky barrier diode?
Metal-semiconductor junction

What is a common use for point-contact diodes?
As an RF detector

In Figure E6-2, which is the schematic symbol for a Schottky diode? **6**	**Figure E6-2** 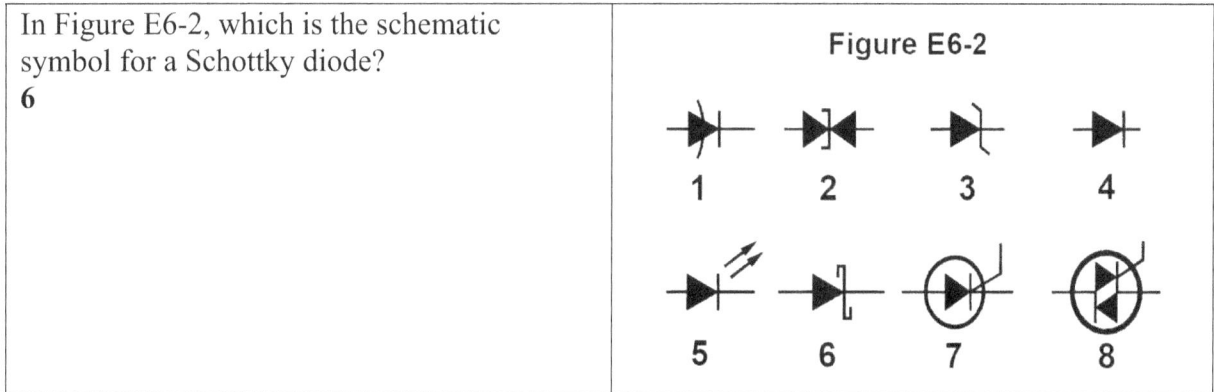

What is used to control the attenuation of RF signals by a PIN diode?
Forward DC bias current

What is the function of hysteresis in a comparator?
To prevent input noise from causing unstable output signals

What happens when the level of a comparator's input signal crosses the threshold voltage?
The comparator changes its output state

What is tri-state logic?
Logic devices with 0, 1, and high-impedance output states

Which of the following is an advantage of BiCMOS logic?
It has the high input impedance of CMOS and the low output impedance of bipolar transistors

Which of the following digital logic families has the lowest power consumption?
CMOS

Why do CMOS digital integrated circuits have high immunity to noise on the input signal or power supply?
The input switching threshold is about half the power supply voltage

What best describes a pull-up or pull-down resistor?
A resistor connected to the positive or negative supply used to establish a voltage when an input or output is an open circuit

| In Figure E6-3, which is the schematic symbol for a NAND gate?
2

In Figure E6-3, which is the schematic symbol for a NOR gate?
4

In Figure E6-3, which is the schematic symbol for the NOT operation (inversion)?
5 | **Figure E6-3**

 |

What is used to design the configuration of a field-programmable gate array (FPGA)?
Hardware description language (HDL)

What is piezoelectricity?
A characteristic of materials that generate a voltage when stressed and that flex when a voltage is applied

What is the equivalent circuit of a quartz crystal?
Series RLC in parallel with a shunt C representing electrode and stray capacitance

Which of the following is an aspect of the piezoelectric effect?
Mechanical deformation of material due to the application of a voltage

Why are cores of inductors and transformers sometimes constructed of thin layers?
To reduce power loss from eddy currents in the core

How do ferrite and powdered iron compare for use in an inductor core?
Ferrite cores generally require fewer turns to produce a given inductance value

What core material property determines the inductance of an inductor?
Permeability

What is the current that flows in the primary winding of a transformer when there is no load on the secondary winding?
Magnetizing current

Which of the following materials has the highest temperature stability of its magnetic characteristics?
Powdered iron

What devices are commonly used as VHF and UHF parasitic suppressors at the input and output terminals of a transistor HF amplifier?
Ferrite beads

What is a primary advantage of using a toroidal core instead of a solenoidal core in an inductor?
Toroidal cores confine most of the magnetic field within the core material

Which type of core material decreases inductance when inserted into a coil?
Brass

What causes inductor saturation?
Operation at excessive magnetic flux

Why is gallium arsenide (GaAs) useful for semiconductor devices operating at UHF and higher frequencies?
Higher electron mobility

Which of the following device packages is a through-hole type?
DIP

Which of the following materials supports the highest frequency of operation when used in MMICs?
Gallium nitride

Which is the most common input and output impedance of MMICs?
50 ohms

Which of the following noise figure values is typical of a low-noise UHF preamplifier?
0.5 dB

What characteristics of MMICs make them a popular choice for VHF through microwave circuits?
Controlled gain, low noise figure, and constant input and output impedance over the specified frequency range

What type of transmission line is often used for connections to MMICs?
Microstrip

How is power supplied to the most common type of MMIC?
Through a resistor and/or RF choke connected to the amplifier output lead

Which of the following component package types have the least parasitic effects at frequencies above the HF range?
Surface mount

What advantage does surface-mount technology offer at RF compared to using through-hole components?
Smaller circuit area
Shorter circuit board traces
Components have less parasitic inductance and capacitance
All these choices are correct

What is a characteristic of DIP packaging used for integrated circuits?
Two rows of connecting pins on opposite sides of package (dual in-line package)

Why are DIP through-hole package ICs not typically used at UHF and higher frequencies?
Excessive lead length

What absorbs the energy from light falling on a photovoltaic cell?
Electrons

What happens to photoconductive material when light shines on it?
Resistance decreases

What is the most common configuration of an optoisolator or optocoupler?
An LED and a phototransistor

What is the photovoltaic effect?
The conversion of light to electrical energy

Which of the following describes an optical shaft encoder?
A device that detects rotation by interrupting a light source with a patterned wheel

Which of these materials is most commonly used to create photoconductive devices?
Crystalline semiconductor

What is a solid-state relay?
A device that uses semiconductors to implement the functions of an electromechanical relay

Why are optoisolators often used in conjunction with solid-state circuits that control 120 VAC circuits?
Optoisolators provide an electrical isolation between a control circuit and the circuit being switched

What is the efficiency of a photovoltaic cell?
The relative fraction of light that is converted to current

What is the most common material used in power-generating photovoltaic cells?
Silicon

What is the approximate open-circuit voltage produced by a fully illuminated silicon photovoltaic cell?
0.5 volts

Which circuit is bistable?
A flip-flop

What is the function of a decade counter?
It produces one output pulse for every 10 input pulses

Which of the following can divide the frequency of a pulse train by 2?
A flip-flop

How many flip-flops are required to divide a signal frequency by 16?
4

Which of the following circuits continuously alternates between two states without an external clock signal?
Astable multivibrator

What is a characteristic of a monostable multivibrator?
It switches temporarily to an alternate state for a set time

What logical operation does a NAND gate perform?
It produces a 0 at its output only if all inputs are 1

What logical operation does an OR gate perform?
It produces a 1 at its output if any input is 1

What logical operation is performed by a two-input exclusive NOR gate?
It produces a 0 at its output if one and only one of its inputs is 1

What is a truth table?
A list of inputs and corresponding outputs for a digital device

What does "positive logic" mean in reference to logic devices?
High voltage represents a 1, low voltage a 0

For what portion of the signal cycle does each active element in a push-pull, Class AB amplifier conduct?
More than 180 degrees but less than 360 degrees

What is a Class D amplifier?
An amplifier that uses switching technology to achieve high efficiency

What circuit is required at the output of an RF switching amplifier?
A filter to remove harmonic content

What is the operating point of a Class A common emitter amplifier?
Approximately halfway between saturation and cutoff

What can be done to prevent unwanted oscillations in an RF power amplifier?
Install parasitic suppressors and/or neutralize the stage

What is a characteristic of a grounded-grid amplifier?
Low input impedance

Which of the following is the likely result of using a Class C amplifier to amplify a single-sideband phone signal?
Signal distortion and excessive bandwidth

Why are switching amplifiers more efficient than linear amplifiers?
The switching device is at saturation or cutoff most of the time

What is characteristic of an emitter follower (or common collector) amplifier?
Input and output signals in-phase

In Figure E7-1, what is the purpose of R1 and R2?
Voltage divider bias

In Figure E7-1, what is the purpose of R3?
Self bias

What type of amplifier circuit is shown in Figure E7-1?
Common emitter

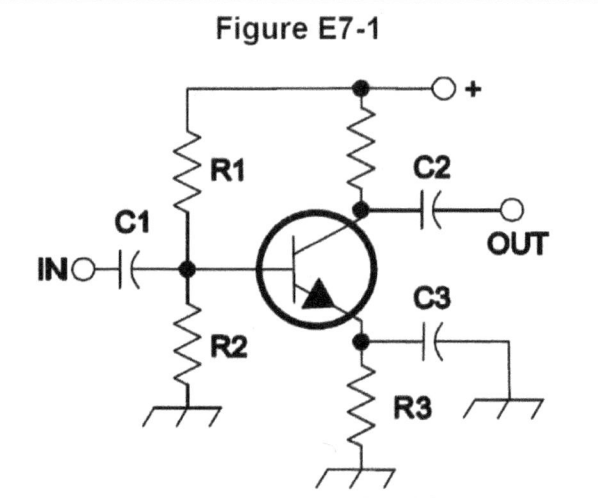

Figure E7-1

How are the capacitors and inductors of a low-pass filter Pi-network arranged between the network's input and output?
A capacitor is connected between the input and ground, another capacitor is connected between the output and ground, and an inductor is connected between the input and output

What is the frequency response of a T-network with series capacitors and a shunt inductor?
High-pass

What is the purpose of adding an inductor to a Pi-network to create a Pi-L-network?
Greater harmonic suppression

How does an impedance-matching circuit transform a complex impedance to a resistive impedance?
It cancels the reactive part of the impedance and changes the resistive part to the desired value

Which filter type has ripple in the passband and a sharp cutoff?
A Chebyshev filter

What are the characteristics of an elliptical filter?
Extremely sharp cutoff with one or more notches in the stop band

Which describes a Pi-L network?
A Pi-network with an additional output series inductor

Which of the following is most frequently used as a band-pass or notch filter in VHF and UHF transceivers?
A helical filter

What is a crystal lattice filter?
A filter for low-level signals made using quartz crystals

Which of the following filters is used in a 2-meter band repeater duplexer?
A cavity filter

Which of the following measures a filter's ability to reject signals in adjacent channels?
Shape factor

How does a linear electronic voltage regulator work?
The conduction of a control element is varied to maintain a constant output voltage

How does a switchmode voltage regulator work?
By varying the duty cycle of pulses input to a filter

What device is used as a stable voltage reference?
A Zener diode

Which of the following describes a three-terminal voltage regulator?
A series regulator

End of Section 4. Rest a bit, relax, and start again when ready.

Part 5 – Read this section for 45 minutes...

Which of the following types of linear voltage regulator operates by loading the unregulated voltage source?
A shunt regulator

What is the purpose of Q1 in the circuit shown in Figure E7-2?
It controls the current to keep the output voltage constant

What is the purpose of C2 in the circuit shown in Figure E7-2?
It bypasses rectifier output ripple around D1

What type of circuit is shown in Figure E7-2?
Linear voltage regulator

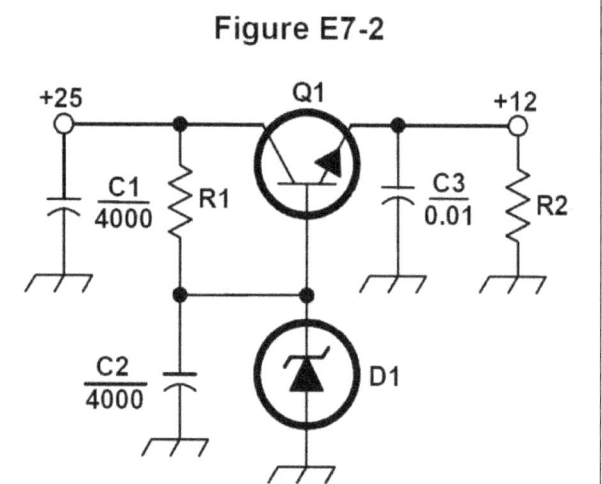

Figure E7-2

How is battery operating time calculated?
Capacity in amp-hours divided by average current

Why is a switching type power supply less expensive and lighter than an equivalent linear power supply?
The high frequency inverter design uses much smaller transformers and filter components for an equivalent power output

What is the purpose of an inverter connected to a solar panel output?
Convert the panel's output from DC to AC

What is the dropout voltage of a linear voltage regulator?
Minimum input-to-output voltage required to maintain regulation

Which of the following calculates power dissipated by a series linear voltage regulator?
Voltage difference from input to output multiplied by output current

What is the purpose of connecting equal-value resistors across power supply filter capacitors connected in series?
Equalize the voltage across each capacitor
Discharge the capacitors when voltage is removed
Provide a minimum load on the supply
All these choices are correct

What is the purpose of a step-start circuit in a high-voltage power supply?
To allow the filter capacitors to charge gradually

Which of the following can be used to generate FM phone signals?
Reactance modulation of a local oscillator

What is the function of a reactance modulator?
Produce PM or FM signals by varying a capacitance

What is a frequency discriminator?
A circuit for detecting FM signals

What is one way to produce a single-sideband phone signal?
Use a balanced modulator followed by a filter

What is added to an FM speech channel to boost the higher audio frequencies?
A pre-emphasis network

Why is de-emphasis used in FM communications receivers?
For compatibility with transmitters using phase modulation

What is meant by the term "baseband" in radio communications?
The frequency range occupied by a message signal prior to modulation

What are the principal frequencies that appear at the output of a mixer?
The two input frequencies along with their sum and difference frequencies

What occurs when the input signal levels to a mixer are too high?
Spurious mixer products are generated

How does a diode envelope detector function?
By rectification and filtering of RF signals

Which type of detector is used for demodulating SSB signals?
Product detector

What is meant by "direct sampling" in software defined radios?
Incoming RF is digitized by an analog-to-digital converter without being mixed with a local oscillator signal

What kind of digital signal processing audio filter is used to remove unwanted noise from a received SSB signal?
An adaptive filter

What type of digital signal processing filter is used to generate an SSB signal?
A Hilbert-transform filter

Which method generates an SSB signal using digital signal processing?
Signals are combined in quadrature phase relationship

How frequently must an analog signal be sampled to be accurately reproduced?
At least twice the rate of the highest frequency component of the signal

What is the minimum number of bits required to sample a signal with a range of 1 volt at a resolution of 1 millivolt?
10 bits

What function is performed by a Fast Fourier Transform?
Converting signals from the time domain to the frequency domain

What is the function of decimation?
Reducing the effective sample rate by removing samples

Why is an anti-aliasing filter required in a decimator?
It removes high-frequency signal components that would otherwise be reproduced as lower frequency components

What aspect of receiver analog-to-digital conversion determines the maximum receive bandwidth of a direct-sampling software defined radio (SDR)?
Sample rate

What sets the minimum detectable signal level for a direct-sampling software defined receiver in the absence of atmospheric or thermal noise?
Reference voltage level and sample width in bits

Which of the following is generally true of Finite Impulse Response (FIR) filters?
FIR filters can delay all frequency components of the signal by the same amount

What is the function of taps in a digital signal processing filter?
Provide incremental signal delays for filter algorithms

Which of the following would allow a digital signal processing filter to create a sharper filter response?
More taps

What is the typical output impedance of an op-amp?
Very low

What is the typical input impedance of an op-amp?
Very high

What is meant by the term "op-amp input offset voltage"?
The differential input voltage needed to bring the open loop output voltage to zero

How can unwanted ringing and audio instability be prevented in an op-amp audio filter?
Restrict both gain and Q

What is the gain-bandwidth of an operational amplifier?
The frequency at which the open-loop gain of the amplifier equals one

What is the frequency response of the circuit in E7-3 if a capacitor is added across the feedback resistor? **Low-pass filter** What voltage gain can be expected from the circuit in Figure E7-3 when R1 is 10 ohms and RF is 470 ohms? **47** What will be the output voltage of the circuit shown in Figure E7-3 if R1 is 1,000 ohms, RF is 10,000 ohms, and 0.23 volts DC is applied to the input? **-2.3 volts** What absolute voltage gain can be expected from the circuit in Figure E7-3 when R1 is 1,800 ohms and RF is 68 kilohms? **38** What absolute voltage gain can be expected from the circuit in Figure E7-3 when R1 is 3,300 ohms and RF is 47 kilohms? **14**	**Figure E7-3** 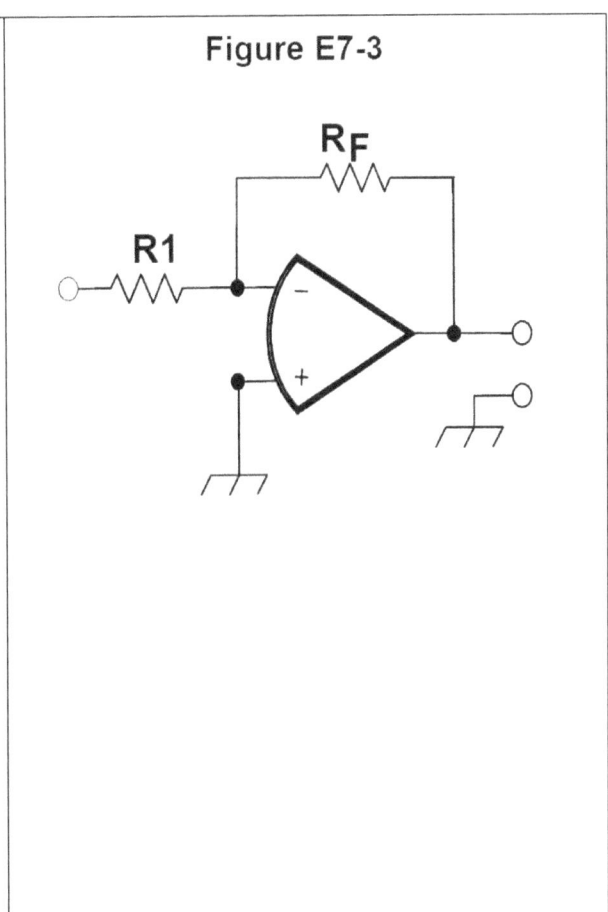

How does the gain of an ideal operational amplifier vary with frequency?
It does not vary with frequency

What is an operational amplifier?
A high-gain, direct-coupled differential amplifier with very high input impedance and very low output impedance

What are three common oscillator circuits?
Colpitts, Hartley, and Pierce

What is a microphonic?
Changes in oscillator frequency caused by mechanical vibration

What is a phase-locked loop?
An electronic servo loop consisting of a phase detector, a low-pass filter, a voltage-controlled oscillator, and a stable reference oscillator

How is positive feedback supplied in a Colpitts oscillator?
Through a capacitive divider

How is positive feedback supplied in a Pierce oscillator?
Through a quartz crystal

Which of these functions can be performed by a phase-locked loop?
Frequency synthesis and FM demodulation

How can an oscillator's microphonic responses be reduced?
Mechanically isolate the oscillator circuitry from its enclosure

Which of the following components can be used to reduce thermal drift in crystal oscillators?
NP0 capacitors

What type of frequency synthesizer circuit uses a phase accumulator, lookup table, digital-to-analog converter, and a low-pass anti-alias filter?
A direct digital synthesizer

What information is contained in the lookup table of a direct digital synthesizer (DDS)?
Amplitude values that represent the desired waveform

What are the major spectral impurity components of direct digital synthesizers?
Spurious signals at discrete frequencies

Which of the following ensures that a crystal oscillator operates on the frequency specified by the crystal manufacturer?
Provide the crystal with a specified parallel capacitance

Which of the following is a technique for providing highly accurate and stable oscillators needed for microwave transmission and reception?
Use a GPS signal reference
Use a rubidium stabilized reference oscillator
Use a temperature-controlled high Q dielectric resonator
All these choices are correct

What technique shows that a square wave is made up of a sine wave and its odd harmonics?
Fourier analysis

Which of the following is a type of analog-to-digital conversion?
Successive approximation

Which of the following describes a signal in the time domain?
Amplitude at different times

What is "dither" with respect to analog-to-digital converters?
A small amount of noise added to the input signal to reduce quantization noise

What is the benefit of making voltage measurements with a true-RMS calculating meter?
RMS is measured for both sinusoidal and non-sinusoidal signals

What is the approximate ratio of PEP-to-average power in an unprocessed single-sideband phone signal?
2.5 to 1

What determines the PEP-to-average power ratio of an unprocessed single-sideband phone signal?
Speech characteristics

Why are direct or flash conversion analog-to-digital converters used for a software defined radio?
Very high speed allows digitizing high frequencies

How many different input levels can be encoded by an analog-to-digital converter with 8-bit resolution?
256

What is the purpose of a low-pass filter used at the output of a digital-to-analog converter?
Remove spurious sampling artifacts from the output signal

Which of the following is a measure of the quality of an analog-to-digital converter?
Total harmonic distortion

What is the modulation index of an FM signal?
The ratio of frequency deviation to modulating signal frequency

How does the modulation index of a phase-modulated emission vary with RF carrier frequency?
It does not depend on the RF carrier frequency

What is the modulation index of an FM phone signal having a maximum frequency deviation of 3000 Hz either side of the carrier frequency if the highest modulating frequency is 1000 Hz?
3

What is the modulation index of an FM phone signal having a maximum carrier deviation of plus or minus 6 kHz if the highest modulating frequency is 2 kHz?
3

What is the deviation ratio of an FM phone signal having a maximum frequency swing of plus or minus 5 kHz if the highest modulation frequency is 3 kHz?
1.67

What is the deviation ratio of an FM phone signal having a maximum frequency swing of plus or minus 7.5 kHz if the highest modulation frequency is 3.5 kHz?
2.14

Orthogonal frequency-division multiplexing (OFDM) is a technique used for which types of amateur communication?
Digital modes

What describes orthogonal frequency-division multiplexing (OFDM)?
A digital modulation technique using subcarriers at frequencies chosen to avoid intersymbol interference

What is deviation ratio?
The ratio of the maximum carrier frequency deviation to the highest audio modulating frequency

What is frequency division multiplexing (FDM)?
Dividing the transmitted signal into separate frequency bands that each carry a different data stream

What is digital time division multiplexing?
Two or more signals are arranged to share discrete time slots of a data transmission

What is Quadrature Amplitude Modulation or QAM?
Transmission of data by modulating the amplitude of two carriers of the same frequency but 90 degrees out of phase

What is the definition of symbol rate in a digital transmission?
The rate at which the waveform changes to convey information

Why should the phase of a PSK signal be changed at the zero crossing of the RF signal?
To minimize bandwidth

What technique minimizes the bandwidth of a PSK31 signal?
Use of sinusoidal data pulses

What is the approximate bandwidth of a 13-WPM International Morse Code transmission?
52 Hz

What is the bandwidth of an FT8 signal?
50 Hz

What is the bandwidth of a 4,800-Hz frequency shift, 9,600-baud ASCII FM transmission?
15.36 kHz

How does ARQ accomplish error correction?
If errors are detected, a retransmission is requested

Which digital code allows only one bit to change between sequential code values?
Gray code

How can data rate be increased without increasing bandwidth?
Using a more efficient digital code

What is the relationship between symbol rate and baud?
They are the same

What factors affect the bandwidth of a transmitted CW signal?
Keying speed and shape factor (rise and fall time)

What is described by the constellation diagram of a QAM or QPSK signal?
The possible phase and amplitude states for each symbol

What type of addresses do nodes have in a mesh network?
Internet Protocol (IP)

What technique do individual nodes use to form a mesh network?
Discovery and link establishment protocols

Why are received spread spectrum signals resistant to interference?
Signals not using the spread spectrum algorithm are suppressed in the receiver

What spread spectrum communications technique uses a high-speed binary bit stream to shift the phase of an RF carrier?
Direct sequence

Which describes spread spectrum frequency hopping?
Rapidly varying the frequency of a transmitted signal according to a pseudorandom sequence

What is the primary effect of extremely short rise or fall time on a CW signal?
The generation of key clicks

End of Section 5. Rest a bit, relax, and start again when ready.

Part 6 – Read this section for 45 minutes...

What is the most common method of reducing key clicks?
Increase keying waveform rise and fall times

What is the advantage of including parity bits in ASCII characters?
Some types of errors can be detected

What is a common cause of overmodulation of AFSK signals?
Excessive transmit audio levels

What parameter evaluates distortion of an AFSK signal caused by excessive input audio levels?
Intermodulation Distortion (IMD)

What is considered an acceptable maximum IMD level for an idling PSK signal?
-30 dB

What are some of the differences between the Baudot digital code and ASCII?
Baudot uses 5 data bits per character, ASCII uses 7 or 8; Baudot uses 2 characters as letters/figures shift codes, ASCII has no letters/figures shift code

What is one advantage of using ASCII code for data communications?
It is possible to transmit both uppercase and lowercase text

What is an isotropic radiator?
A hypothetical, lossless antenna having equal radiation intensity in all directions used as a reference for antenna gain

What is the effective radiated power (ERP) of a repeater station with 150 watts transmitter power output, 2 dB feed line loss, 2.2 dB duplexer loss, and 7 dBd antenna gain?
286 watts

What term describing total radiated power takes into account all gains and losses?
Effective radiated power

Which of the following factors affect the feed point impedance of an antenna?
Antenna height

What does the term "ground gain" mean?
An increase in signal strength from ground reflections in the environment of the antenna

What is the effective radiated power (ERP) of a repeater station with 200 watts transmitter power output, 4 dB feed line loss, 3.2 dB duplexer loss, 0.8 dB circulator loss, and 10 dBd antenna gain?
317 watts

What is the effective isotropic radiated power (EIRP) of a repeater station with 200 watts transmitter power output, 2 dB feed line loss, 2.8 dB duplexer loss, 1.2 dB circulator loss, and 7 dBi antenna gain?
252 watts

Which frequency band has the smallest first Fresnel zone?
5.8 GHz

What is antenna efficiency?
Radiation resistance divided by total resistance

Which of the following improves the efficiency of a ground-mounted quarter-wave vertical antenna?
Installing a ground radial system

Which of the following determines ground losses for a ground-mounted vertical antenna operating on HF?
Soil conductivity

How much gain does an antenna have compared to a half-wavelength dipole if it has 6 dB gain over an isotropic radiator?
3.85 dB

What is the 3 dB beamwidth of the antenna radiation pattern shown in Figure E9-1? **50 degrees** What is the front-to-back ratio of the antenna radiation pattern shown in Figure E9-1? **18 dB** What is the front-to-side ratio of the antenna radiation pattern shown in Figure E9-1? **14 dB**	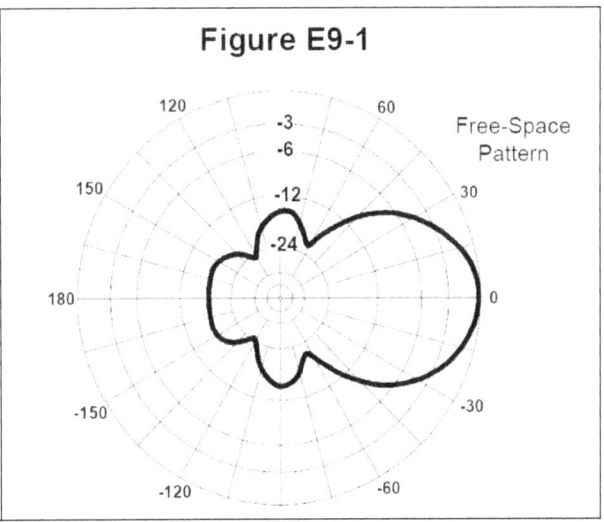 **Figure E9-1**

What is the front-to-back ratio of the radiation pattern shown in Figure E9-2?
28 dB

What type of antenna pattern is shown in Figure E9-2?
Elevation

What is the elevation angle of peak response in the antenna radiation pattern shown in Figure E9-2?
7.5 degrees

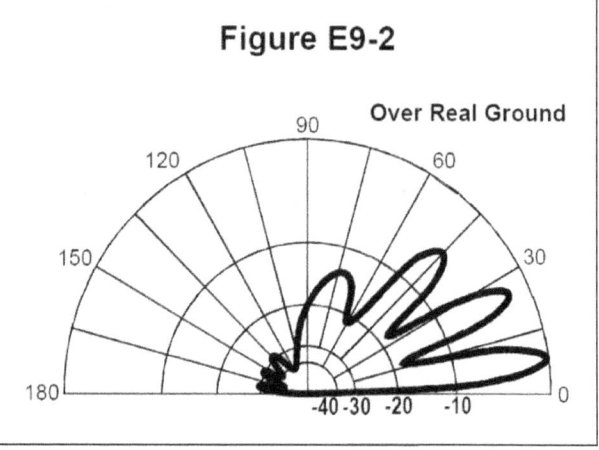

Figure E9-2

What is the difference in radiated power between a lossless antenna with gain and an isotropic radiator driven by the same power?
They are the same

What is the far field of an antenna?
The region where the shape of the radiation pattern no longer varies with distance

What type of analysis is commonly used for modeling antennas?
Method of Moments

What is the principle of a Method of Moments analysis?
A wire is modeled as a series of segments, each having a uniform value of current

What is a disadvantage of decreasing the number of wire segments in an antenna model below 10 segments per half-wavelength?
The computed feed point impedance may be incorrect

What type of radiation pattern is created by two 1/4-wavelength vertical antennas spaced 1/2-wavelength apart and fed 180 degrees out of phase?
A figure-eight oriented along the axis of the array

What type of radiation pattern is created by two 1/4-wavelength vertical antennas spaced 1/4-wavelength apart and fed 90 degrees out of phase?
Cardioid

What type of radiation pattern is created by two 1/4-wavelength vertical antennas spaced 1/2-wavelength apart and fed in phase?
A figure-eight broadside to the axis of the array

What happens to the radiation pattern of an unterminated long wire antenna as the wire length is increased?
Additional lobes form with major lobes increasingly aligned with the axis of the antenna

What is the purpose of feeding an off-center-fed dipole (OCFD) between the center and one end instead of at the midpoint?
To create a similar feed point impedance on multiple bands

What is the effect of adding a terminating resistor to a rhombic or long-wire antenna?
It changes the radiation pattern from bidirectional to unidirectional

What is the approximate feed point impedance at the center of a two-wire half-wave folded dipole antenna?
300 ohms

What is a folded dipole antenna?
A half-wave dipole with an additional parallel wire connecting its two ends

Which of the following describes a G5RV antenna?
A wire antenna center-fed through a specific length of open-wire line connected to a balun and coaxial feed line

Which of the following describes a Zepp antenna?
An end-fed half-wavelength dipole

How is the far-field elevation pattern of a vertically polarized antenna affected by being mounted over seawater versus soil?
Radiation at low angles increases

Which of the following describes an extended double Zepp antenna?
A center-fed 1.25-wavelength dipole antenna

How does the radiation pattern of a horizontally polarized antenna vary with increasing height above ground?
The takeoff angle of the lowest elevation lobe decreases

How does the radiation pattern of a horizontally-polarized antenna mounted above a long slope compare with the same antenna mounted above flat ground?
The main lobe takeoff angle decreases in the downhill direction

How much does the gain of an ideal parabolic reflector antenna increase when the operating frequency is doubled?
6 dB

How can two linearly polarized Yagi antennas be used to produce circular polarization?
Arrange two Yagis on the same axis and perpendicular to each other with the driven elements at the same point on the boom and fed 90 degrees out of phase

What is the most efficient location for a loading coil on an electrically short whip?
Near the center of the vertical radiator

Why should antenna loading coils have a high ratio of reactance to resistance?
To maximize efficiency

Approximately how long is a Yagi's driven element?
1/2 wavelength

What happens to SWR bandwidth when one or more loading coils are used to resonate an electrically short antenna?
It is decreased

What is an advantage of top loading an electrically short HF vertical antenna?
Improved radiation efficiency

What happens as the Q of an antenna increases?
SWR bandwidth decreases

What is the function of a loading coil in an electrically short antenna?
To resonate the antenna by cancelling the capacitive reactance

How does radiation resistance of a base-fed whip antenna change below its resonant frequency?
Radiation resistance decreases

Why do most two-element Yagis with normal spacing have a reflector instead of a director?
Higher gain

What is the purpose of making a Yagi's parasitic elements either longer or shorter than resonance?
Control of phase shift

Which matching system for Yagi antennas requires the driven element to be insulated from the boom?
Beta or hairpin

What antenna matching system matches coaxial cable to an antenna by connecting the shield to the center of the antenna and the conductor a fraction of a wavelength to one side?
Gamma match

What matching system uses a short length of transmission line connected in parallel with the feed line at or near the feed point?
Stub match

What is the purpose of the series capacitor in a gamma match?
To cancel unwanted inductive reactance

What Yagi driven element feed point impedance is required to use a beta or hairpin matching system?
Capacitive (driven element electrically shorter than 1/2 wavelength)

Which of these transmission line impedances would be suitable for constructing a quarter-wave Q-section for matching a 100-ohm feed point impedance to a 50-ohm transmission line?
75 ohms

What parameter describes the interaction of a load and transmission line?
Reflection coefficient

What is a use for a Wilkinson divider?
To divide power equally between two 50-ohm loads while maintaining 50-ohm input impedance

Which of the following is used to shunt feed a grounded tower at its base?
Gamma match

What is the purpose of using multiple driven elements connected through phasing lines?
To control the antenna's radiation pattern

What is the velocity factor of a transmission line?
The velocity of a wave in the transmission line divided by the velocity of light in a vacuum

Which of the following has the biggest effect on the velocity factor of a transmission line?
The insulating dielectric material

Why is the electrical length of a coaxial cable longer than its physical length?
Electromagnetic waves move more slowly in a coaxial cable than in air

What impedance does a 1/2-wavelength transmission line present to an RF generator when the line is shorted at the far end?
Very low impedance

What is microstrip?
Precision printed circuit conductors above a ground plane that provide constant impedance interconnects at microwave frequencies

What is the approximate physical length of an air-insulated, parallel conductor transmission line that is electrically 1/2 wavelength long at 14.10 MHz?
10.6 meters

How does parallel conductor transmission line compare to coaxial cable with a plastic dielectric?
Lower loss

Which of the following is a significant difference between foam dielectric coaxial cable and solid dielectric coaxial cable, assuming all other parameters are the same?
Foam dielectric coaxial cable has lower safe maximum operating voltage
Foam dielectric coaxial cable has lower loss per unit of length
Foam dielectric coaxial cable has higher velocity factor
All these choices are correct

What impedance does a 1/4-wavelength transmission line present to an RF generator when the line is shorted at the far end?
Very high impedance

What impedance does a 1/8-wavelength transmission line present to an RF generator when the line is shorted at the far end?
An inductive reactance

What impedance does a 1/8-wavelength transmission line present to an RF generator when the line is open at the far end?
A capacitive reactance

What impedance does a 1/4-wavelength transmission line present to an RF generator when the line is open at the far end?
Very low impedance

Which of the following can be calculated using a Smith chart?
Impedance along transmission lines

What type of coordinate system is used in a Smith chart?
Resistance circles and reactance arcs

Which of the following is often determined using a Smith chart?
Impedance and SWR values in transmission lines

What are the two families of circles and arcs that make up a Smith chart?
Resistance and reactance

Which of the following is a common use for a Smith chart?
Determine the length and position of an impedance matching stub

On the Smith chart shown in Figure E9-3, what is the name for the large outer circle on which the reactance arcs terminate?
Reactance axis

On the Smith chart shown in Figure E9-3, what is the only straight line shown?
The resistance axis

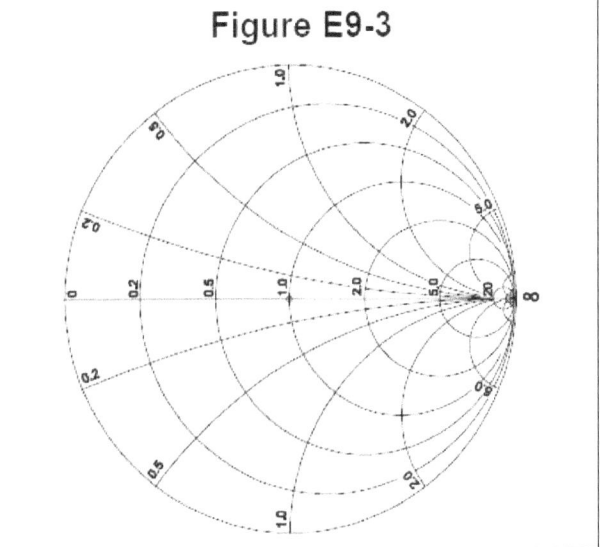

Figure E9-3

How is a Smith chart normalized?
Reassign the prime center's impedance value

What third family of circles is often added to a Smith chart during the process of designing impedance matching networks?
Constant-SWR circles

What do the arcs on a Smith chart represent?
Points with constant reactance

In what units are the wavelength scales on a Smith chart calibrated?
In fractions of transmission line electrical wavelength

When constructing a Beverage antenna, which of the following factors should be included in the design to achieve good performance at the desired frequency?
It should be at least one wavelength long

Which is generally true for 160- and 80-meter receiving antennas?
Atmospheric noise is so high that directivity is much more important than losses

What is receiving directivity factor (RDF)?
Peak antenna gain compared to average gain over the hemisphere around and above the antenna

What is the purpose of placing an electrostatic shield around a small-loop direction-finding antenna?
It eliminates unbalanced capacitive coupling to the antenna's surroundings, improving the depth of its nulls

What challenge is presented by a small wire-loop antenna for direction finding?
It has a bidirectional null pattern

What indicates the correct value of terminating resistance for a Beverage antenna?
Minimum variation in SWR over the desired frequency range

What is the function of a Beverage antenna's termination resistor?
Absorb signals from the reverse direction

What is the function of a sense antenna?
It modifies the pattern of a DF antenna to provide a null in only one direction

What type of radiation pattern is created by a single-turn, terminated loop such as a pennant antenna?
Cardioid

How can the output voltage of a multiple-turn receiving loop antenna be increased?
By increasing the number of turns and/or the area enclosed by the loop

What feature of a cardioid pattern antenna makes it useful for direction-finding antennas?
A single null

What is the primary function of an external earth connection or ground rod?
Lightning charge dissipation

When evaluating RF exposure levels from your station at a neighbor's home, what must you do?
Ensure signals from your station are less than the uncontrolled maximum permissible exposure (MPE) limits

Over what range of frequencies are the FCC human body RF exposure limits most restrictive?
30 - 300 MHz

When evaluating a site with multiple transmitters operating at the same time, the operators and licensees of which transmitters are responsible for mitigating over-exposure situations?
Each transmitter that produces 5 percent or more of its MPE limit in areas where the total MPE limit is exceeded

What hazard is created by operating at microwave frequencies?
The high gain antennas commonly used can result in high exposure levels

Why are there separate electric (E) and magnetic (H) MPE limits at frequencies below 300 MHz?
The body reacts to electromagnetic radiation from both the E and H fields
Ground reflections and scattering cause the field strength to vary with location
E field and H field radiation intensity peaks can occur at different locations
All these choices are correct

What is meant by "100% tie-off" regarding tower safety?
At least one lanyard attached to the tower at all times

What does SAR measure?
The rate at which RF energy is absorbed by the body

Which of the following types of equipment are exempt from RF exposure evaluations?
Hand-held transceivers sold before May 3, 2021

When must an RF exposure evaluation be performed on an amateur station operating on 80 meters?
An evaluation must always be performed

To what should lanyards be attached while climbing?
Tower legs

Where should a shock-absorbing lanyard be attached to a tower when working above ground?
Above the climber's head level

End of Section 6. Rest a bit, relax, and you are ready for the test.